AS Music Listening Tests

OCR

Veronica Jamset

and

Huw Ellis-Williams

RHINEGOLD EDUCATION

www.rhinegoldeducation.co.uk

Music Study Guides
GCSE, AS and A2 Music Study Guides (AQA, Edexcel and OCR)
GCSE, AS and A2 Music Listening Tests (AQA, Edexcel and OCR)
AS/A2 Music Technology Study Guide (Edexcel)
AS/A2 Music Technology Listening Tests (Edexcel)
Revision Guides for GCSE, AS and A2 Music (AQA, Edexcel and OCR)

Also available from Rhinegold Education
Key Stage 3 Listening Tests: Book 1 and Book 2
AS and A2 Music Harmony Workbooks
GCSE and AS Music Composition Workbooks
GCSE Music Literacy Workbook
Writing about Music Workbook
Romanticism in Focus, Baroque Music in Focus, Film Music in Focus, Modernism in Focus, Musicals in Focus
The Immaculate Collection in Focus, *Who's Next* in Focus, *Batman* in Focus, *Goldfinger* in Focus
Music Technology from Scratch
Dictionary of Music in Sound

First published 2011 in Great Britain by
Rhinegold Education
14–15 Berners Street
London W1T 3LJ
www.rhinegoldeducation.co.uk

© 2011 Rhinegold Education
a division of Music Sales Limited

All rights reserved. No part of this publication may be reproduced, stored in a retrieval system,
or transmitted in any form or by any means, electronic, mechanical, photocopying, recording or otherwise,
without the prior permission of Rhinegold Education.

Rhinegold Education has used its best efforts in preparing this guide. It does not assume, and hereby disclaims, any
liability to any party for loss or damage caused by errors or omissions in the Guide
whether such errors or omissions result from negligence, accident or other cause.

You should always check the current requirements of the examination, since these may change. Copies of the OCR
specification may be obtained from OCR Publications, PO Box 5050, Annesley, Nottingham NG15 0DL.
Telephone 0870 870 6622. Fax 0870 870 6621. Email publications@ocr.org.uk.
See also the OCR website at www.ocr.org.uk.

OCR AS Music Listening Tests 3rd Edition
Order Nao. RHG240
ISBN: 978-1-78038-067-4

Exclusive distributors:
Music Sales Ltd
Distribution Centre, Newmarket Road
Bury St Edmunds, Suffolk IP33 3YB, UK

Printed in the EU

Contents

Introduction 5

Section A: Aural Extracts 6

    Instrumental Repertoire 1700–1830 6

    Popular Instrumental Music 1900–Present Day 26

Section B: Prescribed Works 37

    Prescribed Orchestral Scores (June 2012–January 2014) 37

    Jazz 1920–1960 51

        June 2011–January 2013 51

        June 2013–January 2015 57

Answers 63

Full track listing 76

Glossary 79

The authors

Veronica Jamset taught music in primary and secondary schools in both the state and private sections in the West Midlands before taking up her first post in Higher Education as a teacher trainer. She worked in two colleges in Birmingham and then moved to St Mary's College at Strawberry Hill in Twickenham, where she became principal lecturer in music and director of in-service and continuing education. She has been an examiner at various levels since 1990 and, until 2000, was chief examiner for OCR's AS and A-level music syllabuses. She was a member of the team that drafted OCR's current AS/A2 music specification and continues to work as an examiner, reviser and syllabus developer.

Huw Ellis-Williams was brought up in Bangor and studied in Oxford and Exeter. A pianist, organist and part-time composer, he teaches at a comprehensive school in north Wales where he is head of sixth form. Huw has a particular interest in instrumental music of the early 20th century, and in music for theatre and film. He is an examiner for OCR, and is a co-author of the Rhinegold Education OCR AS and A2 Music Study Guides.

Acknowledgements

The authors would like to thank the consultant Sally Ellerington and the Rhinegold Education editorial and design team of Harriet Power and Ben Smith for their expert support in the preparation of this book.

Audio tracks

A CD containing recordings of all the extracts used in this book is available to buy separately from Rhinegold Education (ISBN 978-1-78038-125-1, RHG242).

Copyright

The publisher and authors are grateful for permission to reproduce the following copyright material:

Hawaii Five-O. Music by Mort Stevens. © Copyright 1969 Aspenfair Music Incorporated, USA. Sony/ATV Harmony. All Rights Reserved. International Copyright Secured.

The Newhart Theme. Music by Henry Mancini. © Copyright 1984 TCF Music Publishing Incorporated/FFM Publishing, USA/Hollyweed Music Inc. EMI Music Publishing Limited. All Rights Reserved. International Copyright Secured.

The Ipcress File. Words & Music by John Barry. © Copyright 1965 USI A Music Publishing, USA. Universal/MCA Music Limited. All rights in Germany administered by Universal/MCA Music Publ. GmbH. All Rights Reserved. International Copyright Secured.

Thunderbirds. Music by Barry Gray. © Copyright 1965 ATV Music Limited. Sony/ATV Music Publishing. All Rights Reserved. International Copyright Secured.

The Magnificent Seven. Music by Elmer Bernstein. © Copyright 1960 EMI United Catalogue Inc., USA. EMI United Partnership Limited. All Rights Reserved. International Copyright Secured.

The publisher and authors are grateful to Blue Note Records, Classic FM, Deutsche Grammophon, Etcetera, Hyperion, Living Era, Naïve, Naxos, Phillips Classics, Silva Screen Records and Sony who have granted permission for the use of their recordings.

Introduction

This book contains practice tests and advice for the **three** different types of aural extract that you will have to answer questions about in the examination paper: Introduction to Historical Study in Music. In the exam you will be given your own copy of the CD containing the extracts, which you will be allowed to listen to as many times as you wish on a personal stereo player with headphones. The exam lasts two hours in all, but you may not write during the first 15 minutes. This is called 'Preparation time' and the best use for you to make of it is to sort out which tracks relate to which extract, to listen to each of them carefully at least once and to make a start on identifying the features referred to in the questions.

> The practice tests in this book will help you get used to the sort of questions that might be asked, but if you know you are not certain about some basic areas of musical knowledge (like keys, chords and intervals, or ornamentation) then you might find it helpful to look at the *Rhinegold Dictionary of Music in Sound*.

The first extract, in Section A of the question paper, will come from a piece of instrumental music that you are not expected to be familiar with. You have a choice of **either** Extract 1A, taken from the period 1700–1830 **or** Extract 1B, popular music from 1900 to the present day. Each **extract** will be worth 30 marks.

> For practice tests relating to Extract 1A turn to page 14, or for Extract 1B go to page 27.

In Section B there will be two further extracts, without any choice: Extract 2 (25 marks) will come from one of the 18th- and early 19th-century Prescribed Orchestral Scores that you have studied, and Extract 3 (15 marks) from one of your Prescribed Jazz Recordings.

> For practice tests relating to Extract 2 turn to page 39, and for Extract 3 go to page 51.

Answering the questions on Extract 1 will probably take the longest amount of time but, in the actual examination, try not to spend more than 40 minutes on it – remember that there is also Section C (20 marks) in which you will have to write a short essay. When you begin to work your way through the practice tests in this book don't worry about how long the first ones take you to complete. Treat them more as examples to learn from than timed tests. You will get quicker as you practise.

Section A

Whichever extract you choose, it will be accompanied by a skeleton score. It will give you enough information to be able to follow the music as it plays (including CD timings), but will have quite a lot of details missing. You may be asked to notate small sections of the melody or bass; to recognise harmonies, keys, modulations; identify ornaments and explain techniques of varying melodies; or show that you understand how instrumental textures and colouring can contribute to variation processes. Questions in both types of extract will focus on features of the music related to the two Areas of Study: **Tonality** and **The Expressive Use of Instrumental Techniques**.

Instrumental Repertoire 1700–1830

Introduction

The first six tests in this book are all from the first option – instrumental repertoire 1700–1830. Between them they give examples of most types of question that might be set (but not all come up in every test or paper, of course), and are drawn from the whole period and range of repertoire. Tests 1, 3 and 5 are very similar in genre and style to tests in previous examination papers. OCR's specification stipulates that the music from which the extract will be drawn can be taken 'from solo, chamber or orchestral repertoire'. Tests 2 and 6 are from orchestral repertoire, Tests 1, 3 and 5 from chamber music and Test 4 is for a solo instrument (without accompaniment). So far the repertoire used in previous examination papers has been from the Classical period (after 1750), but the six extracts here give you practice over the whole period described in the specification.

> Test 6 is a little harder than any real test might be.

The tests have been arranged roughly in order of difficulty, so it would be sensible to start with Test 1 and work your way through. The following notes prepare you for the sort of questions you will be asked and give some advice on what to listen for.

Melodic dictation

Whenever you are asked to 'complete the melody' the rhythm will usually be given to help you, but in this example by Mozart (taken from the trio section of his Symphony No. 39 in E♭) you should be able to recognise that the second four-bar phrase (bars 5–8) mirrors the rhythm and shape of the first four bars. Listen to **Track 1** and try to complete the melody:

> If you are unsure about these terms you might find it helpful to look at the *Rhinegold Dictionary of Music in Sound*.

The difference is that the second phrase starts a tone higher, then stretches further up and ends on the tonic (E♭). You may also be asked questions about the melody, to identify an ornament such as a turn or an appoggiatura, or to decide which notes are passing notes.

Chord recognition

> It is very common for harmonies to change more quickly immediately before a cadence: the speed at which harmonies change is known as the **harmonic rhythm**.

The harmony to this melody is very simple, consisting of only tonic and dominant chords. In bars 1–6 the bass consists of either a tonic or dominant note on the first beat of each bar. In bars 7–8 the bass moves in crotchets, but still keeps to notes of chords I and V.

Listen to **Track 1** again and try to hear whether the harmony in each bar is tonic or dominant. Place the Roman numerals I and V in appropriate places under the tune (you will sometimes be asked specifically for Roman numerals so you should learn to use them now).

If you are not sure about Roman numerals consult the Rhinegold Education *OCR AS Music Study Guide* (4th edition), page 21.

Cadences

You could probably hear from the way the two four-bar phrases of the tune 'answered' one another that the first phrase ended on an **imperfect cadence**, the second with a **perfect cadence**. If you were in any doubt, the chord progression confirms this:

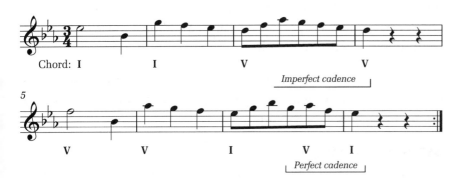

Basically, this is a melody with chordal accompaniment, but there are some interesting details in the scoring which are typical of Mozart's writing for orchestra. The appropriate technical term is **homophonic**: if you are asked to *describe* the texture you may use this word, but make sure you go on to explain what it is that is homophonic about the music.

Texture

To give a full account of the texture you will need to discover 'who does what'. The tune is played by a clarinet. The chords underneath are provided by strings in a crotchet 'oom-pah-pah' rhythm. But the strings are not the only instruments playing the harmony: exactly the same chords are played, in broken form as flowing quavers, by the second clarinet.

Scoring

The 'oom-pah-pah' rhythm is similar to that of a waltz, which was just beginning to become popular in Vienna. It is also characteristic of the **Ländler**, a more rustic Austrian dance.

One further detail: the two phrases of the first clarinet's melody are separated by two crotchet rests (bar 4), but the music is carried forward by a different woodwind instrument which plays an 'echo' in the rests. It does this again in bar 8, joining these eight bars to the next section. Listen again to bars 1–8 to identify this instrument and hear all the other details mentioned above.

Mozart was one of the first composers to use clarinets in a symphony orchestra.

After the repeat the music begins to modulate and, seven bars later, establishes the dominant key with a strong perfect cadence. But, while the strings hang onto the new tonic (the original dominant), two horns are heard clearly for the first time and what they play affects the direction of the music very significantly. Listen to **Track 2** as far as the last pair of notes played by the horns in bar 16 and pause the recording:

Form

In the examination the question paper will always make clear whether repeats are performed in the recorded extract or not.

For a full score of this movement see pages 2–4 of the scores booklet.

What does your ear expect? This typical 'horn call' leads the music straight back to the tonic and the repeat of the opening eight bars.

Variation processes

The complete examination extract will often consist of as many as three short passages from the same piece of music. They will be on separate tracks so that you will not have any difficulty finding where each one begins on your CD. Some of the questions will ask you to compare features between the passages, often with a focus on something that is being repeated but in a varied way: this could be an elaboration of the melody itself but with some intervals or rhythms changed, or different harmony or instrumentation. At other times you might be expected to hear just a short phrase or snatch of rhythm and identify where it first occurred in the extract.

> For the listening tests in this book, the passages for each test will be on the same track, separated by brief pauses.

The passages may be separate variations taken from a formal set, or may be from different sections of a continuous movement, such as the first movement of a symphony.

Mozart

Separate variations

One of the simplest melodies familiar to nearly all of us is *Twinkle, Twinkle, Little Star*. Mozart also knew it as a nursery rhyme in the 18th century but with a French title: *Ah, vous dirai-je, Maman*. He used it as the theme for a set of 12 variations (K. 265) for piano.

> *Ah, vous dirai-je, Maman* was composed in 1781 or 1782 in Vienna. 'K' stands for 'Köchel' who catalogued Mozart's music.

Listen first to the theme (**Track 3**): try to describe its texture. What can you say about its phrase structure? Can you identify the harmonies?

Texture: the accompaniment is as simple rhythmically as the tune itself, mostly note-against-note, creating a two-part texture.

Phrase structure: uncomplicated four-bar phrases in a very basic **ternary** form without modulation:

‖: A (bars 1–8) :‖	‖: B (bars 9–16)	A (bars 17–24) :‖
4+4	4+4	4+4

Harmony: although there are only two parts the **harmonic implications** are clear. In bars 1–4 the **harmonic rhythm** is one chord per bar: I, I, IV, I, but towards the cadence, it quickens to one chord per beat: II–V⁷b, I–VI, IIb–V, I. Then, in bars 9–16, can you hear a repeated G in the bass? The harmonies above it change but it sounds as though it has got 'stuck' on the dominant note. This dominant pedal helps to make our ears 'expect' the return of the A section (rather like the horn call in the previous extract).

> This is a common device in 18th- and early 19th-century music, called a **dominant pedal**.

Four of Mozart's 12 variations are recorded on tracks 4–7. Listen to these tracks as you read the paragraphs below.

Variation 1: Mozart keeps almost the same bass outline, with a few small changes of rhythm, while he fills out the tune with semiquaver patterns of turns, trills and scalic runs. You should still be able to hear the outline of the theme (**Track 4**):

Notice how the notes of the theme hardly ever come on the beat – they are on the second semiquaver (marked +). The dissonances that displace them help to push the music forward.

Variation 2: this is a conversation between treble and bass, sharing new rhythms, but the original outline of both parts is still very clear. In the middle section hear how Mozart fills out the descending steps in the tune with **chromatic passing notes (Track 5)**:

> These are chromatic passing notes because the notes F♯ and E♭ do not belong to the key of C major and there is no modulation to any other key.

Variation 3: there is a complete change of **texture**. The treble changes to three-part chords, with the melody notes at the top, while the bass leaps into life, filling out its harmonic outline with continuous rumbling semiquavers (reminiscent of Variation 1). The effect is thicker and grander. In the middle section treble and bass reverse roles, both starting much lower and gradually rising step-by-step back up to the original pitch. The change of register darkens the texture (**Track 6**).

Variation 4: listen to this variation carefully and try to answer the following questions: What has happened to the key? How many parts are there? What sort of texture is used? How much detail can you describe? (**Track 7**)

> It was usual for all the variations of a theme to be in the same (tonic) key but, towards the middle of a long set, one of the variations might shift to the minor (known as the tonic minor i.e. C major to C minor, here). This helped to vary the colour or mood.

The music is in the tonic minor; there is a new inner part making a contrapuntal or polyphonic texture. Can you hear how the parts imitate each other at the beginning? The chromaticism over the dominant pedal becomes a more persistent feature.

In the first half of the 18th century it was quite common for a set of variations not to use a 'tune' but to be based on a harmonic progression. Handel's *Passacaille* in his Suite No. 7 in G minor takes eight chords in a four-bar sequence as the basis for 15 keyboard variations, which increase steadily in complexity and technical difficulty until a dazzling finish is reached (**Track 8**).

Handel

> Every note in the circle of 5ths is a 5th lower (or a 4th higher) than the previous one. Here Handel gets back to where he started from in seven (diatonic) steps. It is possible, moving through true perfect 5ths chromatically, to pass through every one of the 12 keys.

In the first variation the chords transfer to the treble and the pounding quaver octaves in the bass hammer the progression into our consciousness by filling in the spaces between the true bottom notes: G–C, F–B♭, E♭–A, D–G. This is a segment of the circle of 5ths.

Variations 2, 3 and 4 hang together in a sub-group (as do some other threesomes in this set). They contrast with the theme and Variation 1 by not being chordal, although they pick up on the flowing quaver movement. In **Variation 2** a walking bass in crotchets accompanies a gently flowing quaver line above. The shape of this melodic line makes us aware how easily the harmonic framework lends itself to sequential treatment. In **Variation 3** the roles are reversed (inverted). **Variation 4** continues this line of thought but is busier – the melodic line in the treble is the same as in Variation 2 but the bass now fills out its crotchets as quavers with energetic octave leaps.

> In some sections of the recording on **Track 8** the harpsichordist follows the Baroque convention of playing pairs of quavers in long-short patterns, known as notes inégales (unequal notes).

> Listen to the theme and Variations 1–4 (the first 1:28 of **Track 8**).

Relating three variations to one another in this way counteracts the tendency towards 'bittiness' in variations on such a short foundation. All the variations are designed to show off the harpsichordist's technique and the brilliant sound of the instrument. You don't have to be a keyboard player to recognise how the texture and figuration increase in activity and density as the variations progress. In Variation 12, shortly before his final push to a grand climax, Handel pulls off a conjuring trick with the harmonies – while one hand is busy with intricate semiquavers the other substitutes a chain of diminished 7ths for the original harmonies, making the return of the 'right' harmonies signal that the music is starting on its last lap of the circuit. The final three variations, like variations 2–4, pass a pattern from one hand to the other and then end with both rolling out broken chords in semiquavers simultaneously.

> Listen to the complete set (**Track 8**) and try to note 'who does what' in each, noticing how there are expressive contrasts and the technical brilliance accumulates.

Perhaps the greatest set of variations on a harmonic foundation was the *Goldberg Variations* by Bach. The opening melody may be familiar to you (from its playing in the film *The Silence of the Lambs*), but it is never referred to again in any of the variations until it is played again at the end. It is the harmonic structure, which begins with a descending bass line G, F♯, E, D, B, C, D, G, that provides the material for variation.

> You might try to compose a tune and some variations of your own, using these first eight notes, one per bar, for your bass line. Bach begins in 3/4 and uses a wide range of time signatures for his variations.

Other types of repetition and change

A set of formal variations is not the only sort of repertoire that Extract 1A might be taken from. The repetition of themes or whole passages in an altered form is an essential feature of nearly every instrumental genre between 1700–1830. These include solo and trio sonatas, solo and orchestral suites, and solo and orchestral concertos (concerti grossi) in the Baroque period, together with the many genres which used sonata form (such as sonatas, quartets, trios, and symphonies) in the Classical period.

> Test 6 is from a concerto grosso.

In Baroque concertos an important structural principle was the repetition of the opening section, known as the **ritornello** because it returns throughout the piece. It was often repeated with little change (apart from key or some details of instrumentation in the middle of a movement), but could also occur in a freer, shortened form between **episodes**.

Baroque concertos

The melodic lines in a Baroque movement rarely have the symmetry and balance found in the sort of Classical themes used as the basis for variations (except in some dance forms such as the Minuet). Instead, they seem to unfold, one thought leading to another almost without break, spinning a brief opening idea into a long, winding thread. Listen to **Track 9**, taken from the middle movement of Bach's fourth Brandenburg Concerto and shown in skeleton score below. It uses variation processes, but in different ways from the ones discussed in the first section of this introduction.

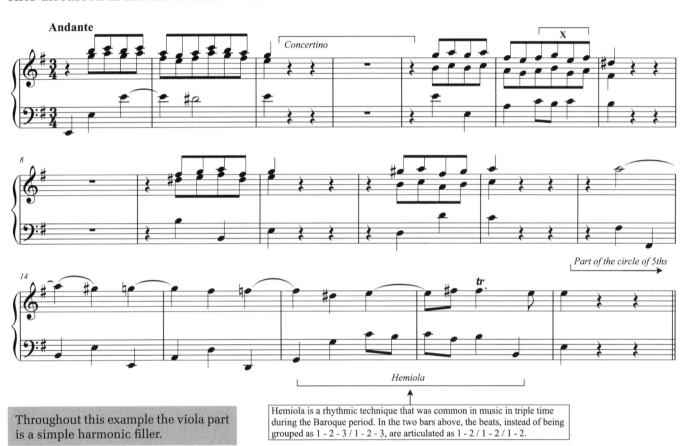

Throughout this example the viola part is a simple harmonic filler.

Hemiola is a rhythmic technique that was common in music in triple time during the Baroque period. In the two bars above, the beats, instead of being grouped as 1 - 2 - 3 / 1 - 2 - 3, are articulated as 1 - 2 / 1 - 2 / 1 - 2.

Bars 1²–3¹: Full orchestra presents the principal idea in a three-part texture – high, flowing quavers in 3rds, with a stark bass line below on the tonic and leading note (I–VII–I in E minor).

All the melodic phrases begin on beat 2 of the bar – the first crotchet in the bass sets the ball rolling.

Bars 3²–5¹: The three soloists in the concertino group (two recorders and a violin) repeat this by themselves in an echo effect. Which of them provides the bass line? At what pitch?

Bars 5²–7¹: The full orchestra moves the melody on, ending with an imperfect cadence. Notice that the first seven quavers are a repetition of the opening but in 6ths (i.e. inverted). The last four quavers (bracketed **X**) form a short pattern that will return later.

A softer repetition of a loud passage was a common technique in Baroque music. **Concertino** is the term used to describe the group of solo instruments in a concerto grosso. **Ripieno** is the term used to describe the accompanying orchestra.

Bars 7²–9¹: Concertino repeats this.

Bars 9²–13¹: Phrase lengths are now reduced to one bar and start to move away from diatonic harmony. Instrumentation, and the alternation of phrases in 3rds then 6ths, is the same as earlier.

> If you are not sure about the circle of 5ths see page 33 in the *OCR AS Music Study Guide* (4th edition) and then ring each new bass note in this extract to make it clear how the bass moves up a 4th every time (which is the same as down a 5th), if you ignore the octave shifts.

Bars 13²–18¹: Full orchestra. Recorder 1, solo and 1st violins make a slow, chromatic descent, dragging their feet with suspensions; the bass line marches stolidly on in crotchets, moving through part of the circle of 5ths.

Thus, after quite a leisurely opening securely in the key of E minor, short phrases have given way to a long, stretched-out phrase that moves adventurously away from the tonic before returning at bars 17–18. What happens in the middle of the texture? Recorder 2 and the 2nd violins keep a tight grip on the original melodic material: their descending sequence uses the cell we have already marked as **X**). Try notating the beginning of this (the first note is F♯) from bars 13²–16.

After this the movement continues to expand organically, always growing from the initial material; towards the end, the concertino refers back to this long sequence but begins it a tone higher. As in previous passages, the solo violin provides the bass line. Listen to this passage on **Track 10** and compare it to the original sequence on **Track 9**. How does it end differently?

Classical sonata form

In sonata-form movements of the Classical and early Romantic periods the development of themes became increasingly important. Techniques of developing melodic or rhythmic cells were not only to be expected in the central section of the movement (the development), but could occur almost anywhere – often in lingering reminiscences of some aspect of a principal theme in the Coda. Developing a theme might take the form of presenting it almost unchanged in a new key, or with slightly altered instrumentation, perhaps shared out in a dialogue between instruments or even in a more rigorously contrapuntal imitative style, or the theme itself might be less easily recognisable.

> A skeleton score is shown on the next page.

Listen to the opening melody of Beethoven's Sixth Symphony, known as the *Pastoral*, on **Track 11**.

> The opening drone bass in 5ths gives the music a rustic flavour right from the outset. Can you hear the 2nd violins, playing a 3rd below the 1st violin from the second quaver of bar 3 to the end of bar 4?

The shape and rhythmic pattern of bars 1 and 2 figure prominently throughout the movement. From bar 5, the motif labelled **a** is treated as a separate figure in its own right. It is also used later in the exposition, from bar 54 (see skeleton score), as part of a modulating transition passage (listen to **Track 12**). Beethoven's developing technique takes one bar of the principal theme (motif **a**), using it in a sequence, repeating it with different harmonies and gradually changing its intervals in a way that is clearly moving towards something new. Can you identify the chords and rhythms omitted from the score in bars 57, 61 and 63?

> See page 63 for answers.

Bars 151–196 on the skeleton score (**Track 13**) is a substantial passage from the central development section of the movement. This time motif **b** (the second bar of the main theme) dominates in repetitions, sequences, varied orchestration, changing harmonies, and is eventually shortened to just its last two notes, the repetitions of which lead to a full statement of the main theme.

Questions on the two or three short passages that make up Extract 1A in the listening paper may ask you to describe or explain how a melody, rhythm or short figure in one of them is presented differently in another. Although you are not expected to be able to discuss these techniques in relation to the prescribed repertoire of Section B, practise spotting them in all the pieces you are studying. This will not only improve your ability to answer questions in Section A, it might also give you some ideas for your own composing work.

Motifs **a** and **b** feature extensively throughout this movement. Motif **c** (which starts at bar 424) which you can hear on **Track 14** is also used but less prominently. Here it stretches out at the end of the theme (in B♭ major), leading towards something new.

On the score above, 'X 8/4/3' indicates how many times that bar is repeated on the recording.

14 Instrumental Repertoire 1700–1830

Test 1   **Track 15**

This extract is part of a movement from a trio by Beethoven. The recording consists of three passages (**Passages 1i, 1ii and 1iii**) separated by brief silences. A skeleton score is printed on pages 5–6 of the scores booklet.

Passage 1i (bars 0–16)

1. Name the woodwind instrument that enters at bar 4^2.

   .... (1)

2. Identify examples of each of the following being used in the first half of Passage 1i (bars $0–8^2$). Give the precise bar and beat number for each of your examples and state whether you are referring to the melody or the accompaniment:

   (a) A chromatic passing note .... (1)

   > A chromatic passing note is a note that does not belong to the current key and passes by step between two harmony notes: they are often easy to spot because of the accidental (a natural, flat or sharp) that precedes them but you will need to check the key because accidentals also occur in minor keys and when a passage has modulated to a new key.

   (b) An acciaccatura .... (1)

   > If you are not sure about any of the principal ornaments, learn them now (they are clearly explained on page 64 of the *OCR AS Music Study Guide* (4th edition) and the glossary at the back of this book).

3. What device is used in bars $8^2–10^2$? (Tick one box.)

   Imitation ☐   Ostinato ☐   Pedal ☐   Sequence ☐   (1)

4. Describe the music played by the piano in the treble of bars $12^2–14^1$.

   ....

   .... (2)

5. (a) What is the key of the theme? .... (1)

   (b) In the second half of Passage 1i (bars $8^2–16$) where is a perfect cadence in the dominant key heard? Give the number of the bar in which the cadence occurs and name the key.

   Bar number ....   Key .... (2)

   (c) Identify the chord marked **X** at bar 15^2 .... (2)

6. Comment on the phrasing and structure of Passage 1i.

   ....

   ....

   ....

   .... (4)

Passage 1ii (bars 16²–48²)

7. Describe **two** ways in which the melody in the treble of bars 16²–20 is a variation of the first four bars of Passage 1i.

   ....

   .... (2)

8. Give a full account of the ways in which the composer has changed the instrumentation in this passage. Refer precisely to bar and beat numbers in your answer.

   | Which instruments are used? Where? What do they play? |

   ....

   ....

   ....

   .... (4)

Passage 1iii (bars 48²–56)

9. **On the score** complete the upper part in bars 53–54. (The rhythm is indicated above the stave.) (4)

10. (a) Identify **one** example in which the melodic line of Passage 1iii shows close similarity to Passage 1i. Give precise bar and beat numbers and explain the resemblance.

    ....

    .... (2)

    (b) Explain briefly how the texture of this passage differs from Passage 1ii.

    ....

    .... (2)

11. In which bar in Passage 1iii does the chord progression Ic–V occur?

    Bar .... (1)

    (Total 30 marks)

> Beethoven originally wrote this music as a Septet (Op. 20) for violin, viola, cello, double bass, clarinet, bassoon and horn. He arranged it in this Trio form in 1803. You might find it helpful to listen to a recording of the original version on **Track 16**. Identify the sound of each instrument and try to hear how Beethoven combines them and varies the scoring.

16 Instrumental Repertoire 1700–1830

Test 2   **Track 17**

This extract is part of a movement from a symphony by Mozart. The recording consists of three passages (**Passages 1i, 1ii and 1iii**) separated by brief silences. A skeleton score is printed on pages 7–10 of the scores booklet.

Passage 1i (bars 1–42)

1. (a) Describe the phrase structure of the melody in bars 1–9^2.

   > How many phrases are there? How similar are they? The crotchet rests give you some clues.

   ....

   ....

   .... (2)

   (b) What is the key of the music at the start of the passage (bars 1–9)?

   > Think about the viola chords in bars 1–3 and the bass line in bars 7–9.

   .... (1)

2. **On the score** complete the bass line in bars 11–12. (The rhythm is indicated below the stave.) (2)

   > Get your bearings by listening to the bass notes in bars 10 and 13.

3. Compare the melody of bars 20^4–28^1 with that of bars 1^4–9^1.

   > Is there a difference?

   ....

   ....

   .... (2)

4. (a) What key has the music reached at bar 28?

   .... (1)

   (b) What is the relationship of this key to the tonic key?

   .... (1)

5. **On the score** complete the melody in bars 38^3–40^2. (The rhythm of the passage is shown below the stave.) (4)

   > Listen to the whole passage in bars 34–42.

Passage 1ii (bars 43–79)

6. Describe the texture of the music in bars 54⁴–63³.

   > Which instruments have the main theme? What do the others play?

   ....
   ....
   .... (2)

7. Compare the music played by the strings in bars 63⁴–74³ with the passage from bars 54⁴–63³.

   > What happens to the main theme?

   ....
   ....
   ....
   .... (4)

Passage 1iii (bars 80–102)

8. What type of scale is played in bar 85? .... (1)

9. **On the score** identify the chords marked **X**, **Y** and **Z** by writing Roman numerals (and inversion letters if needed) in the boxes under the stave. (5)

10. Describe the relationship between the woodwind instruments in the passage from bars 86–98.

    > Texture? Who plays what?

    ....
    ....
    .... (3)

11. In what ways is the music of Passage 1iii related to the music of Passages 1i and 1ii?

    ....
    .... (2)

(Total 30 marks)

Test 3

Track 18

This extract is part of a movement from a string quartet by Haydn. The recording consists of three passages (**Passages 1i, 1ii and 1iii**), separated by brief silences. A skeleton score is printed on pages 11–12 of the scores booklet.

> A standard string quartet usually consists of four instruments: two violins, a viola and a cello.

Passage 1i (bars 0^2–18^2)

The skeleton score of Passage 1i shows the music played by violin 1 and cello.

1. The tonic key is D minor. Bars 6–8 are in F major.

    (a) What is the relationship of this new key to the tonic key?

    .... (1)

    (b) On the score, in the three boxes under the stave in bar 7, write the appropriate Roman numerals to identify the chords **X**, **Y** and **Z**. (6)

    > Remember to indicate inversions and the presence of any 7ths.

2. To what key does the music briefly modulate in bars 8^2–10^2?

    .... (2)

3. **On the score** complete the melody played by violin 1 in bars 13^2–15^1. The rhythm of each note is given above the stave to help you. (4)

4. Identify the form of this passage and give a brief account of its phrasing and structure, commenting on any features of interest.

    Form .... (1)

    Phrasing and structure ....

    .... (2)

Passage 1ii (bars 18²–36²)

The skeleton score shows only the parts for violin 2 and cello.

5. Compare the music played by the cello in this passage with what it played in Passage 1i. Mention pitch, rhythm and articulation, and refer precisely to bar and beat numbers in your answer.

    Pitch ....

    .... (2)

    Rhythm ....

    ....

    .... (3)

    Articulation .... (1)

6. Describe **two** different features of the music played by violin 2 that the viola imitates in this passage. Refer to precise bar and beat numbers in your answer.

    ....

    ....

    ....

    .... (4)

7. Which of the following best describes the role of the crotchet E in bar 36? (Tick one box.)

    Acciaccatura ☐   Appoggiatura ☐   Passing note ☐   Turn ☐ (1)

Passage 1iii (bars 36²–44)

The skeleton score shows only the parts for violin 2 and viola.

8. Briefly describe the music played by violin 1 in bars 37²–44.

    ....

    .... (2)

9. Explain how bars 37²–44 are related to bars 1–8 in Passage 1i.

    .... (1)

(Total 30 marks)

20 Instrumental Repertoire 1700–1830

Test 4

Track 19

This extract consists of a theme followed by seven of Nicolo Paganini's 11 variations for solo violin. On the recording the first part of the theme, and of each variation, is repeated. A skeleton score is printed on pages 13–14 of the scores booklet.

Theme (bars 1–12)

1. (a) What cadence is suggested in bars 3–4?

   .... (1)

   (b) What device is used in the passage from bars 5–8?

   .... (1)

Variation 1 (bars 13–24)

2. Explain the relationship between the theme and this variation. Give **two** examples to illustrate your answer. Identify your examples precisely by reference to bar and beat numbers.

   ....

   ....

   .... (3)

Variation 2 (bars 25–36)

3. In variation 2 which of the following ornaments is used on the second beat of every bar? (Tick one box.)

   Acciaccatura ☐   Appoggiatura ☐   Trill ☐   Turn ☐ (1)

Variation 3 (bars 37–48)

4. Variation 3 is played in octaves. Only the upper note is given in the skeleton score.

   (a) **On the score** complete bars 39–40. (4)

   (b) **On the score** circle one example of a chromatic passing note in the passage from bars 41–48. (1)

   (c) Explain how bar 48 differs from bar 12.

   ....

   .... (2)

Variation 4 (bars 49–60)

5. What type of descending scale is used in bars 49, 51, 53 and 55?

   .... (1)

Variation 5 (bars 61–72)

6. In variation 5 the violinist uses a technique known as 'double stopping'.

    (a) What interval is played in bars 61–64?... (1)

    (b) What interval does this change to at bar 65?... (1)

Variation 6 (bars 73–84)

7. **On the score** complete the lowest part in bars 74 and 75. (4)

All variations

8. If you were to add an accompaniment to the theme and these seven variations, where might you use the chord progression below?

    A⁷   Dm   G⁷   C

    Answer by placing the four chord letters **on the score** underneath any four consecutive bars in the extract where you think the progression would harmonise well. (4)

9. The tempo on this recording is not the same all the way through. Choose **one** example where the performer makes an interpretative choice to get slower or quicker. Identify your example clearly and explain what happens.

    ....

    .... (2)

10. Paganini wrote these variations to show off different aspects of his own exceptional violin-playing technique. Explain **two** ways in which the music of this extract exploits the instrument in a virtuosic way. Refer precisely to bar numbers in your answer.

    ....

    ....

    ....

    .... (4)

(Total 30 marks)

Test 5

Track 20

This extract is part of a theme and variations movement composed by Schubert. The recording consists of three passages (**Passages 1i, 1ii and 1iii**) separated by brief pauses. A skeleton score is printed on pages 15–17 of the scores booklet.

Passage 1i (bars 1–16)

1. Briefly describe the structure of the melody.

   > How many bars long are the phrases? Are all of them the same? You may use labels (such as A and B) but don't forget to describe the phrases as well.

   ....

   .... (2)

2. How does the scoring of the melody in bars 1–8 change when it is repeated?

   > Think about pitch as well as which new instrument starts to play.

   ....

   .... (2)

3. (a) Which of the following best describes the role of the quaver D (marked **X**) in bar 8^2? (Tick one box.)

   Accented passing note ☐   Acciaccatura ☐   Appoggiatura ☐   Mordent ☐ (1)

   (b) **On the score**, in the correct position, write the sign for the ornament heard on the quaver C in bar 15. (1)

4. **On the score** complete the bass part in bars 9^2–12^1. The rhythm of the passage is shown above the stave. (4)

5. The following chords occur in bar 15: Ic (C/G), II (Dm), IIb (Dm/F), V^7 (G^7). (4)

   On the score write the chord name or number for each one in the order they occur under the stave.

   > You first need to work out which notes are the harmony ones in the melody.

Passage 1ii (bars 16^2–32)

6. (a) Describe the music played by the 1st and 2nd violins in bars 17–24.

   1st violin:

   ....

   .... (2)

   2nd violin:

   .... (1)

(b) What performance technique does the viola use in bars 17–20?

.... (1)

7. Explain **two** ways in which the music of Passage 1ii is a variation of Passage 1i and give an example of each.

   > Be careful: the question is about the music, not the scoring.

   ....
   ....
   ....
   .... (4)

Passage 1iii (Bars 32²–48)

8. What is the key of the music at the start of Passage 1iii?

   .... (1)

9. Briefly describe the music played by the clarinet in bar 42.

   > Listen to the violin melody in the bar before (bar 41).

   .... (1)

10. **On the score** complete the 1st violin melody in bars 43–44. (4)

11. Compare this variation with Passage 1ii and explain how it contrasts (apart from its new key).

    ....
    .... (2)

(Total 30 marks)

Test 6

Track 21

This extract is part of a movement from a concerto grosso by J. S. Bach. The recording consists of three passages (**Passages 1i, 1ii and 1iii**) separated by brief pauses. A skeleton score is printed on pages 18–20 of the scores booklet.

> The speed of the extract is quite fast and the music is very busy. Take some time to get used to the pace of Passage 1i. If you find it hard to keep up with the semiquavers on the upper stave, try focusing on the quavers in the bass line. This will also help you hear the harmonic outline.

Passage 1i (bars 1–17)

1. What is the tonic key of the passage? .... (1)

2. The following three chords are used in the passage between bars 8–12:

   II (Gm)   Vb (C⁷/ E)   VI (Dm)

   On the score write these three chords on the first beat of the bar in which each chord occurs. (3)

   > You may use either form of notation for the chords here.

3. **On the score** complete the melody in bar 14. (4)

4. A short trill (*tr*) is heard three times in this passage. **On the score** insert the sign above one note which is ornamented in this way. (1)

5. What is the correct technical term for the device in the melody in bars 8–11? (Tick one box.)

   Inversion ☐   Pedal ☐   Sequence ☐   Syncopation ☐ (1)

Passage 1ii (bars 18–48)

6. (a) In what key does the music in the printed passage end (bar 41)?

   .... (1)

   (b) Name **two** *other* keys used in this passage and state their relationship to the tonic key of the whole extract.

   Key 1 .... Relationship ....

   Key 2 .... Relationship .... (4)

7. What is the relationship of bars 19–31 to the music of Passage 1i?

   ....

   .... (2)

8. What is the function of the note marked **X** in bar 31? (Tick one box.)

    Accented passing note ☐   Acciaccatura ☐

    Appoggiatura ☐   Unaccented passing note ☐   (1)

9. **On the score** complete the bass part in bar 35. (The rhythm is indicated below the stave.)   (4)

10. Describe the music played by the oboes in the following passages:

    (a) Bars 22–29

    ....

    .... (2)

    (b) After the printed score ends (bars 42–48)

    .... (1)

Passage 1iii (bars 49–62)

11. Compare the scoring of the passage from bars 49–52 with the beginning of Passage 1i (bars 1–4).

    ....

    .... (2)

12. (a) Comment briefly on the harmony of bars 57–60^1.

    ....

    .... (2)

    (b) What harmonic device is heard from bars 60^1–62?

    .... (1)

(Total 30 marks)

Popular Instrumental Music 1900–Present Day

Introduction

The five listening tests which follow are designed to give you practice for the **Extract 1B questions**. The OCR specification states that this extract will be 'part of a piece of popular music, taken from 1900 to the present day.' It also lists the 'aural perception skills' which are tested in Section A. The same list of skills is used for both Extract 1A and Extract 1B.

The tests in this book follow the style of the specimen assessment materials from OCR and the questions from past papers for unit G353 of this specification. They use extracts from light popular music, often film or TV themes influenced by popular idioms, rather than examples of jazz or rock music.

You will develop many of the aural skills which you need through the study of the Prescribed Orchestral Scores and Jazz Recordings for Section B. Your composing work will help to develop your understanding of notation, tonality and harmony. The questions are designed to test your listening skills, including describing what you hear, comparing how a composer has used material in different passages, and filling in short passages of pitch or rhythm missing from the skeleton score. You are expected to use appropriate technical language to describe music, using largely the same vocabulary as for Extract 1A.

Orchestral Instruments You will need to identify the names of standard orchestral instruments, including percussion. Be specific when you can. For example, 'drums' is too vague – do you mean 'drum kit' (which includes drums and cymbals) or a particular drum ('snare drum', 'floor tom', 'bass drum')? Practise identifying the instruments you hear and describing the music they play: the flute melody, tremolo chords in the violins, off-beat pizzicato in the double basses. Most of the time you will be expected to describe or compare the music, for which identifying the instrument may only be part of the answer.

The bracketed mark at the end of the question is a clue to how many points the examiner is expecting you to make. Refer to the Answers section at the back of this book to help you think about the level of detail you will need in your examination answers.

Dictation You will be required to complete missing bars of melody, bass or rhythm. You should be familiar with notation in both treble and bass clefs. Take time to learn both clefs if you do not use them in your own performing. In notating pitch you should practise identifying and writing the correct intervals in a melody or bass. You will gain some credit for notating the overall shape of a phrase and for writing correct intervals, even if the pitches are incorrect.

Popular Instrumental Music 1900–Present Day 27

Test 1

Track 22

This extract is taken from *Hawaii Five-O* by Morton Stevens. The recording consists of three passages (**Passages 1i, 1ii and 1iii**) separated by brief silences. A skeleton score is printed on pages 21–22 of the scores booklet.

Passage 1i (bars 1–21)

1. Which rhythm is used for the drum fill in bar 1? (Tick one box.)

   Quavers ☐   Semiquavers ☐   Triplets ☐   Demisemiquavers ☐   (1)

2. Which percussion instrument plays the notes written in the score in bars 2–4?

   ....   (1)

3. (a) Describe the tambourine rhythm played throughout most of Passage 1i.

   | There are two marks for this question, so more than one point needs to be made. |

   ....

   .... (2)

   (b) Give the number of one bar in which the tambourine does not play.

   Bar ....   (1)

4. The following chords are used in the section from bar 13 to bar 17. **On the score** indicate where these chords occur by writing in the boxes provided.

   | Listen to the bass. There are other clues in the printed melody part. |

   I (Cm)   IV (F)   V (G)   ♭VI (A♭)   (4)

5. **On the score** complete the trumpet melody from bar 14² to the end of bar 15. The rhythm is printed above the stave.   (5)

6. Which held note is played by the horns in bar 21? Write your answer on the score.   (1)

Passage 1ii (bars 22–38)

7. Compare the instrumentation and texture of Passage 1i (bars 5–20) with Passage 1ii.

   ....

   ....

   ....

   ....

   .... (5)

28 Popular Instrumental Music 1900–Present Day

Passage 1iii (bars 39–62)

8. What instrument plays the melody in bars 39–47?

   .... (1)

9. **On the score** complete the bass guitar part in bars 46–47. The rhythm of the bass part is indicated above the stave. (3)

10. **On the score** write the rhythm of the brass chords played in bars 48–49. (2)

11. Identify the devices used in the following places:

    > Device means a technique of composing, not a technique of performing.

    (a) Melody in bars 54–59 .... (1)

    (b) Bass guitar in bars 55–59 .... (2)

    (c) Woodwind/brass chords in bars 60–61 .... (1)

    (Total 30 marks)

Test 2

Track 23

This extract is taken from the title music for *Newhart* by Henry Mancini. The recording consists of three passages (**Passages 1i, 1ii and 1iii**) separated by brief silences. A skeleton score is printed on pages 23–24 of the scores booklet.

Passage 1i (bars 1–21)

1. In bars 1–4:

    (a) What technique is used in the harp part?

    .... (1)

    (b) Which tuned percussion instrument can be heard?

    .... (1)

2. The following chords are used in the section from bars 5–7. **On the score** indicate where these chords occur by writing in the boxes provided.

    IV (B♭)   I (F)   VI (Dm)   V⁷d (C/B♭)   (4)

3. **On the score** complete the violin melody from bars 9–11. The rhythm is printed above the stave. (5)

4. What is the key of the music at the following places?

    (a) Bar 13 .... (1)

    (b) Bar 17 .... (1)

5. What device is used in the bass at bars 17–18?

    .... (1)

Passage 1ii (bars 22–33)

6. Describe the texture from bar 26 to the end of Passage 1ii.

    > Don't use words such as 'thick' or 'thin'. Describe how the instruments are used or combined.

    .... (1)

7. Name the ornament used in the trumpet part at bar 33.

    .... (1)

Passage 1iii (bars 34–55)

8. Compare the structure of Passage 1iii with Passage 1i and Passage 1ii.

   ....

   ....

   ....

   ....

   .... (5)

9. Describe the main features of the music (not the instruments) in bars 54–55.

   > Detailed points needed here, but there are no marks for identifying the instruments that are playing.

   ....

   ....

   ....

   ....

   .... (5)

10. **On the score** complete the bass guitar part in bars 46–47. The rhythm is printed above the stave. (4)

(Total 30 marks)

Test 3

Track 24

This extract is taken from the title music for *The Ipcress File* by John Barry. The recording consists of two passages (**Passages 1i and 1ii**), separated by brief silences. A skeleton score is printed on pages 25–27 of the scores booklet.

Passage 1i (bars 1–42)

1. Describe the structure of the passage.

   > Hint: structure is often described in letter style. For example, AAB, AB.

   .... (1)

2. **On the score** write in bar 1 the rhythm used in the accompaniment (xylophones or tuned percussion) from bar 1 to bar 18. (2)

3. Name the key in the following bars:

   (a) Bar 3 .... (1)

   (b) Bar 23 .... (1)

4. **On the score** complete the cimbalom melody in bars 13–16. The rhythm of the melody is indicated above the stave. (5)

   > A cimbalom is a Hungarian instrument played by striking metal strings tuned to fixed pitches.

5. Describe how the rhythm of the music changes at bars 19–26.

   ....

   ....

   .... (3)

Passage 1ii (bars 43–101)

6. (a) Which instrument plays the repeated motif printed in bars 43–54?

   .... (1)

   (b) How is the sound of the instrument modified?

   .... (1)

   (c) Which instrument takes over the motif at bar 55?

   .... (1)

7. Describe how the theme from Passage 1i (bars 3–18) is used in bars 54–86 of Passage 1ii. Refer to bar numbers in your answer.

> Compare the two versions of the melody. Remember you have at least six points to get into this space.

....

....

....

....

....

.... (6)

8. Identify the cadence in bars 66–67.

> Remember to answer cadence questions with the name of the cadence, not Roman numerals.

.... (1)

9. Give the location of the following features which are added to the printed melody in bars 71–83.

    (a) Mordent   bar ....   beat .... (1)

    (b) Accent   bar ....   beat .... (1)

    (c) Glissando   bar .... (1)

10. In which bars is the motif printed in bars 83–86 previously heard in this passage?

    Bars .... (1)

11. **On the score** complete the bass part in bars 87–89¹. The rhythm is printed above the stave. (3)

(Total 30 marks)

Test 4

Track 25

This extract is taken from the original television soundtrack for *Thunderbirds* by Barry Gray. The recording consists of two passages (**Passages 1i and 1ii**), separated by brief silences. A skeleton score is printed on pages 28–29 of the scores booklet.

Passage 1i (bars 1–28)

1. **On the score** write the rhythm of the snare drum in bar 1. (3)

2. Describe the structure of this passage.

   ....

   .... (2)

3. Use the table below to describe the instrumentation and texture in bars 5–8, and to show how the instrumentation and texture changes in bars 9–10.

Instrumentation and texture bars 5–8	Changes in bars 9–10

(6)

4. **On the score** complete the melody in bars 23–24. The rhythm is printed above the stave. (5)

5. Describe the harmony at the end of the passage (bars 21–28).

   ....

   ....

   ....

   .... (4)

Passage 1ii (bars 29–42)

6. How is the melodic material from Passage 1i used in Passage 1ii?

   ....

   .... (2)

7. **On the score** write the appropriate notation where the following features appear in the violin part:

   (a) a trill (1)

   (b) tremolo (1)

   > Don't write 'trill' or 'tremolo' – use the notation the violin players would expect to see.

8. What instruments play the melody in:

   (a) Bars 33–34? .... (1)

   (b) Bars 36–37? .... (1)

9. Describe how the composer creates a feeling of contrast in the music in bars 39–40.

   ....

   ....

   ....

   .... (4)

   (Total 30 marks)

Popular Instrumental Music 1900–Present Day

Test 5 Track 26

This extract is taken from the music for *The Magnificent Seven* by Elmer Bernstein. The recording consists of three passages (**Passages 1i, 1ii and 1iii**) separated by brief silences. A skeleton score is printed on pages 30–31 of the scores booklet.

Passage 1i (bars 1–33)

1. **On the score** write the rhythm of the chords in bars 1–2. (2)

2. Compare the instrumentation of bars 6–18 and bars 20–32.

   ....

   ....

   ....

   ....

   .... (5)

3. (a) **On the score** complete the bass part in bars 16–17. The rhythm of the bass is indicated above the stave. (2)

   (b) Identify the cadences used in:

   (i) Bars 17^3–18^1 ....

   (ii) Bars 31^3–32^1 .... (2)

4. The following chords are used in the section from bars 22–28. **On the score** indicate where these chords occur by writing in the boxes provided.

   I (E♭)   II (Fm)   IV (A♭)   V^7 (B♭^{7}) (4)

Passage 1ii (bars 34–46)

5. Name the percussion instrument added at the beginning of Passage 1ii.

   .... (1)

6. **On the score** complete the melody in bars 37–39 and bars 41–43. The rhythm is printed above the stave. (5)

7. Compare the structure of the melody in Passage 1ii and bars 6–18.

   ....

   ....

   .... (3)

8. Name the playing technique used in each of the following places:

   (a) The guitar in bars 34–35.

   .... (1)

   (b) The trumpet in bar 42.

   .... (1)

Passage 1iii (bars 47–73)

9. What percussion instrument is added at the beginning of Passage 1iii?

   .... (1)

10. Give **three** differences in the way in which musical material from Passages 1i and 1ii is treated in this passage.

    ....

    ....

    .... (3)

(Total 30 marks)

Section B: Prescribed Works

In this section of the listening paper you will be asked questions about two of the six pieces of music you have studied closely. The first extract (labelled **Extract 2** on the question paper) will be taken from one of the Prescribed Orchestral Scores; the second (labelled **Extract 3** on the question paper) will come from one of the three Prescribed Jazz Recordings you have studied.

> Check the specification or the *OCR AS Music Study Guide* (4th edition) to make sure that you study the correct list of works for the year and session in which you are sitting the examination.

Extract 2

Your CD will contain **two** recordings of the same extract, made by different orchestras. You will be given a copy of the notated score of the extract. It may not look exactly the same as the scores that you have been using – the layout may be slightly different and the bar numbering will only refer to the extract, not the whole piece – but it will contain all the notes and performance instructions such as expression marks and articulation signs. You are not allowed to take your own copy of the score into the examination room. The questions on this extract are worth 25 marks.

The questions will ask about the music itself and the way it is performed. You should make sure, therefore, that you are thoroughly familiar with the sound of the music and understand all of the composer's performing instructions. If you can, it would also be helpful, once you know the music reasonably well from one recording, to listen to another to see if you can spot the differences. Sometimes these are very obvious, such as one recording using a large orchestra and the other using a smaller one, perhaps with period instruments, but others can be quite subtle changes of tempo, phrasing or dynamics. You will usually be asked, as well, to explain which part of the whole movement the extract belongs to: you should therefore try to understand the overall structure, particularly features of the music such as keys which may change depending on, for instance, whether an extract is drawn from an exposition or a recapitulation (in sonata form). Take notice of details of scoring – which instruments play what – and changes of texture: you might be asked to compare the extract with some other part of the movement, for which you will have to rely on your memory.

The first few questions on Extract 2 usually focus on details of the notation and may ask you to explain the meanings of signs or abbreviations such as the bowing instructions to strings *pizz.* and *arco*. Make sure that you understand the terms *div.* and *a 2*: these are frequently used to tell performers which of them is to play at any particular moment. There will probably be a question as well about the notation itself: for this you need to be able to read the alto and tenor clefs, and to understand the principle on which transposing instruments such as clarinets in A or horns in D are notated – you will almost certainly be asked to turn a short passage into sounding-pitch equivalents. This is something that you can practise and it is worth doing so to make sure that you don't take

> The *OCR AS Music Study Guide* (4th edition) gives lots of practice in doing this in the exercises on each piece.

too long over it in the examination.

Another skill that you can practise is identifying chords and keys. Being confident about clefs and transposing instruments will help you in this because reading all the notes at one particular moment in an orchestral score can be quite challenging.

At least one question will involve comparing aspects of the two recorded performances. The more familiar you are with the composer's phrasing, expression and articulation markings, the more comfortable you are likely to be with this. Get into the habit of noticing interpretative details such as small changes of tempo, how the strings attack notes marked staccato, or a crescendo and diminuendo not marked in the score but introduced by the conductor.

As well as memorising the meaning of signs, symbols and abbreviations and practising your reading skills, the most important preparation is listening to the music itself, again and again, trying to hear more detail of the scoring each time.

Prescribed Orchestral Scores

Test 1 Tracks 27 and 28

This extract is taken from the first movement of Vivaldi's Concerto in E minor for Bassoon and Orchestra, RV 484. The scores booklet contains a full score of this extract on pages 32–33. Two recordings of the extract from different performances are provided on the CD: Extract 1A (**Track 27**) and Extract 1B (**Track 28**).

1. Identify the ornaments written in the score at the following points:

   (a) bar 2^2 in the bassoon .... (1)

   (b) bar 8^3 in the bassoon .... (1)

   (c) bars 11^3 and 11^4 in the 2nd violin .... (1)

2. (a) Name the key at the beginning of the extract (bar 1).

   .... (1)

   (b) Name the key at the end of the extract (bar 11).

   .... (1)

3. Explain the use of the terms 'Solo' in the cello part in bar 1 and 'Tutti' in bar 11.

   ....

   .... (2)

4. Describe the relationship between the solo bassoon part and the accompaniment from bars 1^2–10^1.

   ....

   ....

   ....

   ....

   ....

   .... (6)

5. Compare the two performances of this music and comment on the similarities and differences between them. You may wish to refer to such aspects as:

   ➤ Pitch
   ➤ Timbre
   ➤ Ornamentation
   ➤ The realisation of the continuo.

   ....
   ....
   ....
   ....
   ....
   ....
   ....
   ....
   ....
   .... (8)

6. (a) Relate the printed extract to the overall structure of the movement from which it is taken.

   ....
   .... (2)

   (b) Describe briefly how the solo bassoon makes use of melodic material heard from earlier in the movement.

   ....
   .... (2)

(Total 25 marks)

OCR AS Music Listening Tests scores booklet

Introduction

Trio from Mozart Symphony No. 39

Tracks 1 and 2

4 Introduction

The above repeat is not observed on the recording

Instrumental Repertoire 1700–1830

Test 1　　　　　　　　　　　　　　　　　　　　　　　　　　Track 15

6 Instrumental Repertoire 1700–1830

Passage 1iii

Complete the melody

Test 2

Track 17

Passage 1i

Test 3   Track 18

Passage 1i

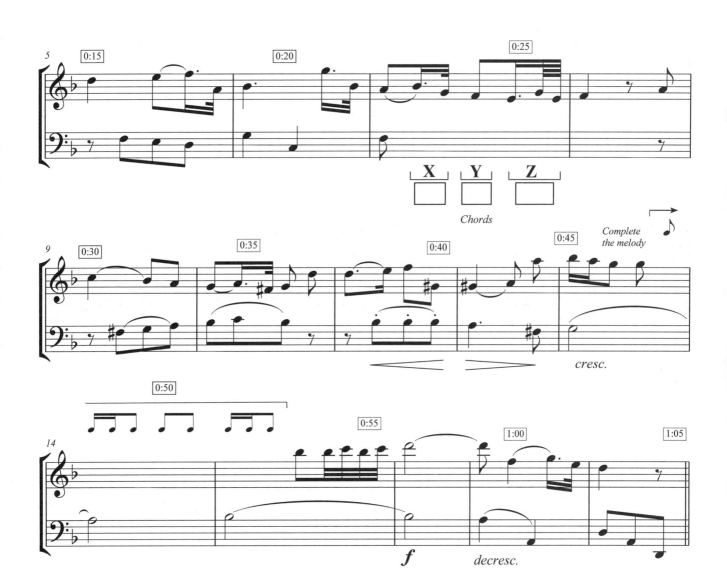

Passage 1ii

12 Instrumental Repertoire 1700–1830

Passage 1iii

Test 4

Track 19

Test 5

Track 20

Passage 1i

Passage 1ii

(The horn sounds an octave lower than notated here.)

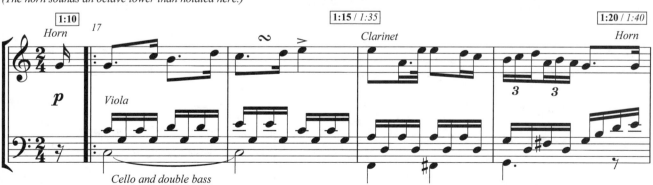

Instrumental Repertoire 1700–1830

18 Instrumental Repertoire 1700–1830

Test 6   Track 21

Passage 1i

Passage 1ii

Complete the bass part

20 Instrumental Repertoire 1700–1830

The music continues for seven more bars

Passage 1iii

Popular Instrumental Music 1900–Present Day

Test 1   Track 22

Passage 1i

Passage 1ii

22 Popular Instrumental Music from 1900 – Present Day

Passage 1iii

Test 2   Track 23

Passage 1i

Passage 1ii

24 Popular Instrumental Music from 1900 – Present Day

Passage 1iii

Complete the bass part

Test 3 Track 24

Passage 1i

26 Popular Instrumental Music from 1900 – Present Day

Passage 1ii

28 Popular Instrumental Music from 1900 – Present Day

Test 4

Track 25

Passage 1i

Popular Instrumental Music from 1900 – Present Day

Passage 1ii

30 Popular Instrumental Music from 1900 – Present Day

Test 5   Track 26

Passage 1i

Popular Instrumental Music from 1900 – Present Day 31

Passage 1ii

Passage 1iii

Prescribed Orchestral Scores

Test 1   Tracks 27 and 28

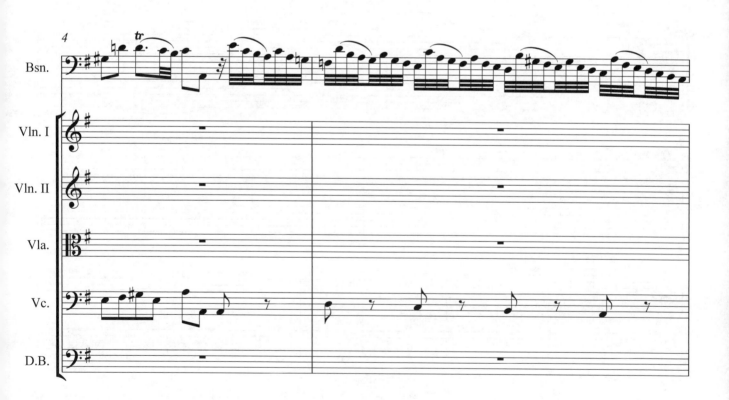

Test 2 Tracks 29 and 30

Test 3 Tracks 31 and 32

Test 4

Tracks 33 and 34

Prescribed Orchestral Scores 45

Test 5   Tracks 35 and 36

Prescribed Orchestral Scores 49

Test 6 Tracks 37 and 38

Prescribed Orchestral Scores 53

Prescribed Orchestral Scores 41

Test 2   **Tracks 29 and 30**

This extract is taken from the first movement of Vivaldi's Concerto in E minor for Bassoon and Orchestra, RV 484. The scores booklet contains a full score of this extract on pages 34–36. Two recordings of the extract from different performances are provided on the CD: Extract 2A (**Track 29**) and Extract 2B (**Track 30**).

1. Describe briefly the features of the solo bassoon part in bars 1–4.

   ....

   .... (2)

2. (a) Identify the composing device used in bars 5–7.

   .... (1)

   (b) Identify the chord used at bar 5^1.

   .... (1)

   (c) What is the harmonic function of the note G at bar 5^3?

   .... (1)

   (d) Which performing technique is used in the 1st violin at bar 15^1?

   .... (1)

3. On the stave below write out the viola part in bars 13–16^1 **in the treble clef**. (4)

4. Describe the writing for the orchestra (not the solo part) at the end of the extract (bars 12–16^1).

   ....

   ....

   ....

   .... (4)

5. Relate the tonality of this extract to the tonality of the movement from which it is taken.

   ....

   ....

   .... (3)

6. Compare the two performances of this music and comment on the similarities and differences between them. You may wish to refer to such aspects as:

   ➢ The interpretation of the bassoon solo
   ➢ Period and modern performance
   ➢ The role of the harpsichord
   ➢ The balance of the recording.

   ....
   ....
   ....
   ....
   ....
   ....
   ....
   ....
   ....
   .... (8)

(Total 25 marks)

Test 3

Tracks 31 and 32

This extract is taken from the fourth movement of Haydn's *Drum Roll* Symphony No. 103 in E♭ major, Hob. I:103. The scores booklet contains a full score of this extract on pages 37–42. Two recordings of the extract from different performances are provided on the CD: Extract 3A (**Track 31**) and Extract 3B (**Track 32**).

1. Identify the key (tonality) at the beginning of the extract.

   .... (1)

2. Explain the following terms used in the printed extract:

   (a) a2 (bassoons at bar 31)

   .... (1)

   (b) 𝄐 (at bar 47)

   .... (1)

3. Describe the relationship between the strings and the woodwind in bars 2–30.

   ....

   ....

   .... (3)

4. On the stave below write the clarinet parts in bars 25–30 **at sounding pitch**. (4)

5. Compare the two performances of this music and comment on the similarities and differences between them. You may wish to refer to such aspects as:

   ➢ Tempo
   ➢ Balance
   ➢ Articulation.

   ....

   ....

   ....

   ....

   ....

44 Prescribed Orchestral Scores

....

....

....

....

.... (8)

6. Describe the tonality at the end of the extract.

   ....

   .... (2)

7. Describe briefly the music that immediately follows the recorded extract.

   ....

   .... (2)

8. Relate the printed extract to the overall structure of the movement from which it is taken.

   ....

   ....

   .... (3)

(Total 25 marks)

Test 4

Tracks 33 and 34

This extract is taken from the fourth movement of Haydn's *Drum Roll* Symphony No. 103 in E♭ major, Hob. I:103. The scores booklet contains a full score of this extract on pages 43–46. Two recordings of the extract from different performances are provided on the CD: Extract 4A (**Track 33**) and Extract 4B (**Track 34**).

1. (a) Explain the following terms used in the printed extract:

    (i) a2 (horns at bar 5)

    .... (1)

    (ii) *fz* (strings and woodwind at bar 14)

    .... (1)

    (b) Explain the notation in the timpani at bars 27–32.

    .... (1)

2. On the stave below write out the horn parts in bars 1–4 **at sounding pitch**. (4)

3. Describe the textures and orchestration in the passage between bars 1–18¹.

    ....
    ....
    ....
    ....
    ....
    .... (6)

4. Explain the harmony and tonality in bars 19–26.

    ....
    .... (2)

46 Prescribed Orchestral Scores

5. Compare the two performances of this music and comment on the similarities and differences between them. You may wish to refer to such aspects as:

    ➢ Pitch
    ➢ Balance of instrumental parts
    ➢ Dynamics.

    ....

    ....

    ....

    ....

    ....

    ....

    ....

    ....

    ....

    .... (8)

6. Relate the printed extract to the overall structure of the movement from which it is taken.

    ....

    .... (2)

(Total 25 marks)

Test 5

Tracks 35 and 36

This extract is taken from the first movement of Beethoven's Concerto in D major for Violin and Orchestra, Op. 61. The scores booklet contains a full score of this extract on pages 47–50. Two recordings of the extract from different performances are provided on the CD: Extract 5A (**Track 35**) and Extract 5B (**Track 36**).

1. Explain the meaning of the following terms:

   (a) *dolce* (bar 1 solo violin)

   .... (1)

   (b) **sf** (bar 22^4 oboe and clarinet)

   .... (1)

   (c) *poco cresc.* (bar 28 strings)

   .... (1)

2. On the stave below write the clarinet parts in bars 2–5 **at sounding pitch**. (3)

3. Explain how Beethoven uses harmony and tonality in this passage.

   ....
   ....
   ....
   .... (4)

4. Comment on the writing for the solo violin in bars 30–35.

   ....
   ....
   .... (3)

5. Compare the two performances of this music and comment on the similarities and differences between them. You may wish to refer to such aspects as:

   ➢ Tempo
   ➢ The solo violin part
   ➢ The overall sound of each recording.

   ....
   ....
   ....
   ....
   ....
   ....
   ....
   ....
   ....
   .... (8)

6. (a) Relate the printed extract to the overall structure of the movement from which it is taken.

   ....
   .... (2)

   (b) Describe briefly the music that precedes this extract.

   ....
   .... (2)

   (Total 25 marks)

Test 6

Tracks 37 and 38

This extract is taken from the first movement of Beethoven's Concerto in D major for Violin and Orchestra, Op. 61. The scores booklet contains a full score of this extract on pages 51–56. Two recordings of the extract from different performances are provided on the CD: Extract 6A (**Track 37**) and Extract 6B (**Track 38**).

1. Explain the following terms used in the printed extract:

   (a) **sfp** (oboes and horns at bar 10)

   .... (1)

   (b) a2 (woodwind at bar 27)

   .... (1)

   (c) *sempre* **ff** (strings and bassoons at bar 30)

   .... (1)

2. Identify the principal features of the solo violin melody in bars 1–12.

   ....

   ....

   .... (3)

3. On the stave below write the clarinet parts in bars 24–26 **at sounding pitch**. (4)

4. Show how Beethoven creates a dramatic and expressive effect in the orchestral tutti passage in bars 19–32. Refer to the use of the orchestra and to harmony and tonality in your answer.

   ....

   ....

   ....

   ....

   .... (5)

5. Compare the two performances of this music and comment on the similarities and differences between them. You may wish to refer to such aspects as:

   ➢ The orchestra in the two performances
   ➢ Dynamics and expression
   ➢ The interpretation of the solo part
   ➢ The quality of the recorded sound.

   ....

   ....

   ....

   ....

   ....

   ....

   ....

   ....

   ....

   .... (8)

6. Explain the notation of the solo violin part at the end of the recorded extracts (at bar 32^3).

   ....

   .... (2)

   (Total 25 marks)

Jazz 1920–1960

Prescribed works June 2011–January 2013

Test 1 Track 39

This extract is taken from *Alligator Crawl* performed by Louis Armstrong and His Hot Seven. It consists of one chorus.

1. Describe briefly the texture of the music in this chorus.

   ....

   ....

   .... (3)

2. The extract is taken from the second chorus of *Alligator Crawl*. Give **two** ways in which this chorus is different from the first chorus.

   ....

   .... (2)

3. Complete the table below by listing features prominent in the music played by the instruments in this extract.

Instrument	Prominent features of the music played
Trumpet	
Clarinet	
Trombone	

   (5)

4. (a) Name the clarinet player in this extract. .... (1)

   (b) In which year was this music recorded? .... (1)

5. Describe briefly the music that immediately follows the recorded extract.

   ....

   ....

   .... (3)

(Total 15 marks)

Test 2

Track 40

This extract is taken from *Alligator Crawl* performed by Louis Armstrong and His Hot Seven. The extract consists of a passage for solo trumpet.

1. Who is the trumpeter in this recording?

   .... (1)

2. Outline the main features of the accompaniment.

   ....

   ....

   ....

   ....

   .... (5)

3. (a) Comment on the shape of the trumpet melody. Explain how the melody in the extract is developed and varied.

   ....

   ....

   ....

   .... (4)

   (b) Which performing technique is used on the final note of the recorded extract?

   .... (1)

4. Describe briefly the music that immediately follows the recorded extract.

   ....

   ....

   .... (3)

5. In which city was this performance recorded?

   .... (1)

(Total 15 marks)

Test 3

Track 41

This extract is taken from *Ko-Ko* performed by Charlie Parker. It consists of one chorus.

1. Describe how this extract is typical of the bebop style of jazz.

   ....

   ....

   .... (3)

2. Name the drummer heard in this extract.

   .... (1)

3. Describe the compositional devices used in the B section of this chorus (0:26–0:38).

   ....

   .... (2)

4. How does the accompaniment change in the second half of the extract (0:26–0:51)?

   ....

   .... (2)

5. Describe the features of the music at the end of the extract that indicate this is the end of the chorus.

   ....

   ....

   ....

   ....

   .... (5)

6. Describe briefly the music that immediately follows the recorded extract.

   ....

   .... (2)

(Total 15 marks)

Test 4

This extract is taken from *Ko-Ko* performed by Charlie Parker. The extract is from the beginning of the recording.

1. (a) Identify the trumpet player in this recording.

   .... (1)

   (b) Which instrument from the saxophone family is featured in this music?

   .... (1)

2. Explain the role of the drums in this extract.

   ....
   ....
   .... (3)

3. (a) Name the interval between the two solo parts at the beginning of the extract.

   .... (1)

   (b) Outline the main features of the trumpet and saxophone parts in this extract.

   ....
   ....
   ....
   .... (4)

4. (a) Describe briefly the music that immediately follows the recorded extract.

   ....
   ....
   .... (3)

   (b) Where is the music of this extract heard again in this piece?

   .... (1)

5. In which city was this performance recorded?

   .... (1)

(Total 15 marks)

Test 5

Track 43

This extract is taken from 'It Ain't Necessarily So' from *Porgy and Bess*. The solo is played by Miles Davis. The extract consists of three short choruses.

1. (a) Who is conducting this performance? .... (1)

   (b) Who is playing the bass part? .... (1)

2. Describe the music played by the drums in this extract.

   ....

   ....

   .... (3)

3. (a) Which instruments play the accompaniment figure heard at the beginning of the extract?

   .... (1)

   (b) When was this motif first heard?

   .... (1)

4. Describe **two** features of the solo that are typical of Miles Davis' style of playing.

   ....

   .... (2)

5. The music changes in the last chorus of the extract (0:28–0:43).

   (a) Describe the main features of the music played by the band (not the solo).

   ....

   ....

   .... (3)

   (b) Name **one** difference between this chorus and the first time the chorus is heard.

   .... (1)

6. Describe briefly the music that immediately follows the recorded extract.

   ....

   .... (2)

(Total 15 marks)

56 Jazz 1920–1960

Test 6  Track 44

This extract is taken from 'It Ain't Necessarily So' from *Porgy and Bess* performed by Miles Davis and the Gil Evans Orchestra. The extract is taken from the end of the recording.

1. (a) Which performing technique is used by the double bass in this extract?

   .... (1)

   (b) Explain the ways in which the drums and bass keep time at the beginning of the extract.

   ....

   .... (2)

   (c) Name the drummer in this recording.

   .... (1)

2. Describe the accompaniment figure in the horns at the beginning.

   ....

   ....

   ....

   .... (4)

3. Explain the relationship between the trumpet melody and the accompaniment in this extract.

   ....

   ....

   ....

   ....

   .... (5)

4. In what way is the structure of this extract different to the other choruses in this recording?

   .... (1)

5. In which city was this performance recorded?

   .... (1)

(Total 15 marks)

Prescribed works June 2013–January 2015

Test 1   Track 45

This extract is taken from *Hotter Than That* performed by Louis Armstrong and His Hot Five. The extract consists of a short introduction for piano and one complete chorus.

1. (a) Name the pianist in this recording.

   .... (1)

   (b) Describe briefly the main features of the introduction.

   ....

   .... (2)

2. (a) Identify the solo instrument in the first half of the chorus.

   .... (1)

   (b) Which of the following techniques are used in the solo? (Tick two boxes.) (2)

   Pedal note ☐   Glissando ☐   Plunger mute ☐
   Riff ☐   Scat ☐   Fall-off ☐

3. Explain the changes in texture heard in the chorus section (not the introduction).

   ....

   ....

   ....

   ....

   ....

   .... (6)

4. Describe briefly the music that immediately follows the recorded extract.

   ....

   ....

   .... (3)

(Total 15 marks)

58 Jazz 1920–1960

Test 2 **Track 46**

This extract is taken from *Hotter Than That* by Louis Armstrong and His Hot Five. The extract consists of one chorus for solo trumpet.

1. Identify the instruments that accompany the trumpet solo.

   ....

   .... (2)

2. Comment on the structure and use of harmony in this chorus.

   ....

   .... (2)

3. Describe the main features of the melody and performance of the trumpet solo in this extract.

   ....

   ....

   ....

   .... (4)

4. (a) Relate the recorded extract to the overall structure of the work from which it is taken.

   ....

   .... (2)

   (b) Describe briefly the music that immediately follows the recorded extract.

   ....

   ....

   .... (3)

5. (a) In which city was this performance recorded?

   .... (1)

   (b) Identify the recording company for which this track was made.

   .... (1)

(Total 15 marks)

Test 3

Track 47

This extract is taken from *Koko* performed by Duke Ellington and His Famous Orchestra. The extract consists of two choruses.

1. (a) Identify the solo instrument playing in this extract.

   .... (1)

   (b) How is the sound of the instrument modified?

   ....

   .... (2)

2. Comment on the instruments and textures used in the accompaniment of the first chorus.

   ....

   ....

   ....

   ....

   ....

   .... (6)

3. Identify **two** differences between the first chorus and the second chorus.

   First difference: .... (1)

   Second difference: .... (1)

4. Describe the music that immediately follows the recorded extract.

   ....

   ....

   .... (3)

5. In which year was this music recorded?

   .... (1)

   (Total 15 marks)

Test 4

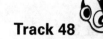
Track 48

This extract is taken from *Koko* by Duke Ellington and His Famous Orchestra. The extract consists of two choruses.

1. (a) Describe briefly the role of the double bass in the first chorus of this extract.

   ....

   .... (2)

   (b) Which performing technique does the double bass use?

   .... (1)

   (c) Identify the double bass player in this recording.

   .... (1)

2. Compare Ellington's use of the brass and reeds in the first chorus with their use in the second chorus.

   ....

   ....

   ....

   ....

   ....

   .... (6)

3. (a) Identify the structure used for the choruses in this extract.

   .... (1)

   (b) How is the tonality of this piece unusual?

   .... (1)

   (c) Relate the recorded extract to the overall structure of the work from which it is taken.

   ....

   .... (2)

4. Identify the city in which this recording was made.

   .... (1)

(Total 15 marks)

Test 5

Track 49

This extract is taken from *Boplicity* performed by Miles Davis and His Orchestra. The extract consists of part of the final chorus.

1. Who is the piano soloist in this recording?

   .... (1)

2. Describe the main features of the piano solo.

   ....

   ....

   ....

   .... (4)

3. Comment on the textures and instruments used in the ensemble section of this extract.

   ....

   ....

   ....

   ....

   ....

   .... (6)

4. (a) Where is the music of the ensemble section heard earlier in the piece?

   .... (1)

   (b) How is the version heard in this extract different from the version played earlier in the piece?

   ....

   ....

   .... (3)

   (Total 15 marks)

Test 6

Track 50

This extract is taken from *Boplicity* performed by Miles Davis and His Orchestra. The extract consists of a passage for solo trumpet and the band.

1. How many players feature in this recording?

   .... (1)

2. Describe briefly the music played by the rhythm section in this extract.

   ....
   ....
   ....
   ....
   .... (5)

3. (a) Compare the relationship between the trumpet solo and the accompaniment (not the rhythm section) at the beginning and the end of the extract.

   ....
   ....
   ....
   .... (4)

   (b) Identify **two** features of the trumpet solo at the end of the extract that are characteristic of Miles Davis.

   ....
   .... (2)

4. Relate the recorded extract to the overall structure of the work from which it is taken.

   ....
   .... (2)

5. In which city was this recording made?

   .... (1)

(Total 15 marks)

Answers

The answers given here are intended as a guide. Alternative answers will always receive credit if they form an accurate and unambiguous response to the precise question posed.

Instrumental Repertoire 1700–1830

Answers to page 12 on Beethoven's Sixth Symphony

Bar 57 – chord vi. This can also be heard in the key to which the music is modulating (the dominant, C major) as the new ii.
Bar 61 also has a dual identity – Ic in the tonic (F major) or IVc in the new key.
Bar 63 confirms the modulation with V⁷b in the new key.
Clarinets, bassoons and horns play these chords in triplet quavers.

Test 1

1. Clarinet.
2. (a) In the accompaniment only: the A♭s in bar 2² or 6²; or the E♮ in bar 3².

   > Bars 3–4 might look like a modulation to the dominant key, F major, but they do not establish a new key. It is, in fact, an imperfect cadence in the tonic key, B♭ major.

   (b) In the melody before the E♭ in bar 3¹ or bar 7¹.
3. Sequence.

   > Bars 9²–10² are the same as bars 8²–9² but a tone lower (except for a small difference in the chord voicing: can you see what this difference is?).

4. It is a long trill; on F; using the notes F and G.
5. (a) B♭ major.
   (b) Bar 12; F major.
   (c) IIb (you may also use the notation Cmin/E♭).
6. The first half (bars 0²–8) consists of two phrases of four bars, each beginning in the same way (the second on the upbeat of bar 4²), the first ending with an imperfect cadence, the second with a perfect cadence, both in the tonic key. This is then repeated. The first four bars of the second half (bars 8²–12²) contrast and modulate to the dominant, passing through G minor in bars 8²–9. The last four bars (bars 12²–16) are a repetition of bars 4²–8, in the tonic key. This structure could be represented as A1 A2 :‖: B A2. All the four-bar phrases consist of two x two-bar units. This is a very typical classical structure.
7. Several possible answers, but the most obvious are: it starts on the same note and the quaver shape of bar 1 is filled out with semiquavers in bar 17; the descending quavers of bar 3 are syncopated in bar 19 and include the original acciaccatura as a strong semiquaver on the first beat of the bar.

   > Did you notice that the question asks you about the melody, not the accompaniment?

8. If you have labelled the structure in question 6 as above, you can use the letters as shorthand for identifying each phrase as you describe it (but you will first have had to notice that Beethoven has written out the repeats in full). Bars 16²–24 = A1 + A2 played by the piano alone. This is repeated in bars 24²–32 but with the cello playing the melody accompanied by the piano. Bars 32²–40 = B + A2 played by piano alone, the melody is then repeated by cello with piano accompaniment in bars 40² to 48. Don't forget to mention that the clarinet is silent.

9.

10. (a) The shape of bar 48² to the B♭ in bar 49 mirrors the opening of the theme.

    (b) It is in two-part counterpoint: the cello begins and is imitated by the clarinet. In some places they play in parallel 10ths. The piano punctuates with chords at the cadences.

11. In bar 52.

Test 2

Beat numbering: the sign ¢ means that the time signature is $\frac{2}{2}$ so Mozart heard these bars in two minim beats, not four crotchets. You will also find it more comfortable to count two beats to a bar as you listen, but we have numbered each bar in four beats to avoid ambiguities.

1. (a) Bars 5⁴–9³ are a repetition of bars 1⁴–5³, but a note lower; a descending sequence; there are two main four-bar phrases; they both consist of two, two-bar phrases; they answer one another (the first two bars end by leaping upwards, the second two bars come back down by step); and the rhythm is the same throughout; all the phrases begin on the last beat of the bar (with an anacrusis).

   > Sometimes a question about structure can be answered by using letters like A, B and C to show which phrases are the same and which ones are different. In this question, though, you really need to describe the most obvious features.

(b) G minor (the tonic chord is heard in bars 1–2 in the lower strings, and the F sharps in bars 7–8 are the leading note that confirms the key.)

> Notice that the melody in bars 3⁴–5 descends in the melodic minor version of the G minor scale, but bars 7⁴–9² use the harmonic minor version.

2.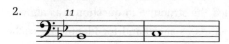

3. The phrase structure is similar; bars 20⁴–24² are an exact repeat but, instead of the sequence starting at bar 24⁴ on a note lower, it starts a note higher than the first phrase.

4. (a) B♭ major.

   (b) Relative major.

5.

> These notes can also be heard leading up to this passage in bars 34–38 and then, after it, in bars 40³–41, the exact melody is repeated but in a quaver pattern.

6. The strings are playing in two parts only; up to bar 59 the first phrase of the main melody (similar to bars 1–5²) is in unison in the lower strings (violas, cellos and basses); from bars 59⁴–63 it is played by upper strings (1st and 2nd violins); the two parts imitate one another (are in dialogue) and their parts get turned upside down (inverted); wind and horns sustain chords.

7. The contrapuntal passage continues from bar 63⁴–67², but the melody starts a note lower each time, in a descending sequence; from bar 69 the repeating melody is reduced from four bars to its second two-bar phrase (the descending scale part of it), remaining now in the upper strings (violins).

> Be very careful: the question is not about texture but about the music, though you may need to mention instruments to describe who does what.

8. (G) harmonic minor.

> Look back at question 1(b). You've already been asked about the key of the music, so in question 8 the answer 'G minor' would not be enough.

9. X = IV; Y = Ic ; Z = V⁷

> You will often be able to use alternative ways of writing chord names (e.g. Gm/B♭ for Ib), but this question has specifically asked you for Roman numerals. Learn these now. Knowing them will help you understand tonality better in your coursework exercises in Section A of your Composing Unit.

10. They are echoing one another; clarinet starts, bassoon answers an octave lower; then flute joins clarinet an octave higher.

11. The first two-bar phrase of the melody from Passage 1i is played by violins at bar 90⁴–92; the head of the tune (the three-note motif) is used in the woodwinds' imitative passage; it was also prominent at the end of Passage 1ii.

The three passages come from the exposition, development and recapitulation sections of the first movement of Mozart's Symphony No. 40 in G minor, K. 550. They all show different aspects of Mozart's treatment of his first subject.

Test 3

1. (a) Relative major.

> The melodic line only implies the modulation (there is no obvious change of accidentals to give a clue). The harmony establishes the new key.

   (b) X = IIb; Y = Ic; Z = V⁷.

2. G minor.

> The F♯s in the melody and bass are the new leading note (7th of the scale). G minor's relationship to the tonic, D minor, is the subdominant.

3.

> This is very straightforward if you hear it as a rising sequential pattern, starting at the end of bar 12.

4. Binary; it is in unequal halves. Bars 1 to 8 = two four-bar phrases which begin similarly but the first phrase cadences perfectly in the tonic key (bar 4²), the second in the relative major. In the second half (bars 9–18) the second phrase is lengthened to six bars by means of a sequence.

> Modulation to the relative major is the standard pattern for a binary melody that begins in a minor key.

5. Pitch: the notes are exactly the same, but there are some changes of octave e.g. bars 8¹ and 26¹.

   Rhythm: some quavers are held longer e.g. the repeated B♭s in bar 11 become a minim in bar 29; longer notes are repeated using notes of shorter value e.g. the minims in bars 13–15 become ♪♪ ↧ ♪ in bars 31–33.

   Articulation: the playing in this passage is more detached.

   > There is only one mark for articulation so this would be a sufficient answer. This aspect of articulation is worth developing your ear for and paying attention to – you will need it in your comparison of interpretations in Section B. The contrast here might almost be described as legato/staccato: in Passage 1i all the notes were held for their full value and some were in small slurred groups; in Passage 1ii, the notes are played in a very detached manner (this is in keeping with the way Haydn has broken up the minims), many cut rather short of their full value.

6. The viola imitates the scales: in bar 22 it plays an ascending scale; in bar 26 a descending scale ahead of violin 2; in bar 28 it imitates immediately after and continues into the next bar with a descending scale. It also imitates, a beat later, the sighing figure which the second violin plays in the ascending sequence in bars 31 to 33.

   > The question asks for different features so your two examples should not both be of scales.

7. Appoggiatura (it delays the final D, clashing with the underlying harmony).

8. Mainly arpeggios (rising and falling); in continuous semiquaver triplets.

   > You are not expected to describe the actual notes and have not been asked to give any examples in this question (it says 'Briefly describe'), but be as precise as you can – just saying something like 'busy' would be too vague.

9. The cello part is exactly the same as in bars 1–8.

   > This set of variations is unusual because the most obvious constant ingredient is not a melody in the highest part but the cello line at the bottom. The first eight bars almost sound Baroque – the quartet was composed in 1772 – and the complex phrase structure is typical of Haydn.

Test 4

1. (a) Imperfect (bar 3 suggests chord I in A minor, bar 4 suggests the dominant i.e. I – V. This becomes clearer as the variations progress e.g. bars 87–88 in variation 7).

   (b) (Descending) sequence.

   > For one mark the answer 'sequence' is sufficient but always be as precise as you can.

2. It has the same harmonic basis (the broken chords outline the harmonies that would fit the melody e.g. bar 1 = chord I (tonic in A minor); bar 2 = chord V (dominant, an E major chord). Or, bars 18–20 match bars 6–8 (D minor, G major, C major chords).

3. Acciaccatura.

4. (a)

   (b) Either the F♯ in bar 42 or the D♯ in bar 44 (not the C♯ in bar 41 – it is a harmony note).

   (c) The A is approached by a crotchet B above (appoggiatura) and the final A is omitted.

5. Chromatic.

6. (a) 3rd (below the given notes).

   (b) 10th (above the given notes).

   > A 10th is an octave plus a 3rd.

7.

8. Bars 5–8 in the theme or the equivalent place in any variation e.g. bars 17–20.

   > The four chords follow a short part of the circle of 5ths, the bass line would go A – D – G – C.

9. In the theme, and all the variations except variation 4, the violinist slows in the final bar, bar-and-half or two bars, sometimes considerably e.g. bar 48. Variation 3 is taken throughout at a slower speed than the rest of the extract and highlights the tendency (also audible elsewhere) to linger slightly on the first beat of each bar: it also has rubato (and slides between notes, a feature worth commenting on in answer to question 10). There are, therefore, many examples for you to choose from.

10. This is not a question that can only be answered by violinists. You will have gained some experience of the sort of music usually played by violinists in this period from your study of orchestral repertoire. You will also be familiar from your own experience as a performer, whether as an instrumentalist or a singer, with the sorts of techniques that present difficulty – especially when playing or singing long stretches of fast notes at a breathless tempo. Some of the techniques have already been flagged in the questions: double-stopping, ornaments, rapid chromatic scales. You may mention these in your answer as evidence of the variety of techniques used in a short span of music, but you will also need to identify at least one other technique yourself: as well as the slides (portamento or glissando) already pointed out in variation 3, there is triple stopping (playing three-note chords) in variation 6, other scales and several different uses made of rapidly descending arpeggios. You might also mention the many wide leaps. You may also have noticed the left-hand pizzicato in variation 7, the simultaneous use of notes that are plucked while others are being bowed. For each technique that you mention remember to point to a specific example e.g. arpeggio and wide leap in bar 60.

> Left-hand pizzicato: you would not be expected to have recognised that this is performed in a different way from normal pizzicato. Instead of the performer putting down his bow and plucking the strings with his right hand, the notes that give the outline are bowed and the others plucked by the left hand as it fingers each one.

Paganini's Variations were transcribed for piano by Liszt; he tried to match the difficulty of the violin techniques with comparable pianistic challenges. Many other composers have written variations on this theme, e.g. Brahms, Rachmaninov, Lutoslawski and Lloyd Webber (for his brother Julian, a cellist).

Test 5

1. Four-bar phrases – A¹ A² :||: B A³

:|| A¹	A² :||:	B	A³ :||
(b 1–4²)	(b 4²–8)	(b 9–12)	(b 12²–16)

All the A phrases begin the same way but have different endings – A1 modulates to the dominant (G major), A2 ends in a perfect cadence in the tonic, A3 stretches the melody to its highest point bar 14²); A2 and A3 both begin on an upbeat semiquaver (anacrusis). (To get two marks it would probably be enough to give an outline structure and to describe one aspect in detail.)

2. The first playing (bars 1–8) is for strings only; on the repeat the clarinet enters and takes the melody at its original pitch; 1st violin doubles it an octave higher.

3. (a) Appoggiatura (it leans onto the C).
   (b) *tr* (the trilling part is quite short and it ends with a turn).

4. [musical notation, bar 10]

5. The correct order is: II IIb Ic V⁷ (This is a very common progression of chords, especially at a cadence point, in classical styles. It would be worth remembering this for use in your Composing Section A coursework exercises.)

6. (a) 1st violin alternates silences with ascending arpeggios and rapid scales.
      2nd violin keeps up a constant repeated pattern of busy demisemiquavers in the middle of the texture.
   (b) Pizzicato (plucked).

7. The melodic outline is similar in many ways e.g. bar 20 follows the shape of bar 4, but the rhythm is very different. Instead of smoothly-flowing semiquavers some notes are held longer and there are many dotted notes (give an example). The high A in bar 14 is held longer in Passage 1ii and descends chromatically. Some of the harmony is the same e.g. bar 19 is the same as bar 3, but cellos and basses hold the first C through bar 17² as a tonic pedal under dominant harmony and the F♯ in the bass is dropped in bar 23. There is more chromaticism in bars 25–26.

8. A♭ major.

9. It echoes what the violin has played in the previous bar but a note higher, almost an exact sequence.

10.

11. Less busy texture with many more sustained notes, smoother semiquavers; generally higher in all parts; melody often in lower strings and the parts are more equal; a more reflective mood.

Test 6

1. F major.

2. II = bar 8; Vb = bar 9; VI = bar 11.

> The harmonic rhythm in this passage begins by being one harmony per bar (bars 1–4), then mostly two harmonies per bar. At cadences the chords change more frequently.

Answers

3.

> It is exactly the same as bar 16 but an octave higher.

4. Any of bars 4², 14⁵ or 16⁵.

5. Sequence.

> Bars 10–11 are exactly the same pattern as bars 8–9, but a step lower.

6. (a) A minor.

> You might ask, 'How could I tell that it was minor and not major?' There is no 3rd – either C♮ or C♯ – in bars 40–41 to decide the matter one way or the other. In Baroque music, modulations are almost always to related keys: A minor, not A major, is related to F major (it is the dominant of the relative minor).

(b) C major = dominant; D minor = relative minor.

> This time the question does not ask you to give bar numbers but always check carefully to see whether they are needed.

7. They are a repeat of bars 5–17; but in C major (or, a 4th lower, or in the dominant); differently scored.

> The question asks about the music so you do not have to give details of instruments used.

8. Accented passing note.

> The harmony note is the next one. Notice that Bach is not afraid of the consecutive 7ths that this causes between the bass and treble parts.

9.

> The bass notes outline the harmonies V–I in A minor (E major chord to A minor chord).

10. (a) They play the horn's melody from bar 8; in a sequence; in (three-part) chords.

    (b) 1st oboe plays the violins' music from bar 21⁴–31¹; the other two accompany with chords (in A minor).

11. Instead of the whole orchestra, only a violino piccolo plays melodically; accompanied by continuo; in two-part counterpoint.

> The violino piccolo was identified at bar 31 in Passage 1ii. It is a small violin, tuned higher than a normal one.

12. (a) The bass outlines part of the circle of 5ths (F – B♭ – E – A – D – G – C).

> This would be a sufficient answer to get both marks. Only pointing out that it is sequential would be worth one mark

(b) Dominant pedal.

Popular Instrumental Music 1900–Present Day

Test 1

1. Semiquavers.

2. Timpani.

3. (a) Repeated quavers, accenting the second and fourth beats of the bar.

    (b) Bar 1 or bar 5.

4. Bar 13: V (G); bar 14: I (Cm); bar 16: IV (F); bar 17: ♭VI (A♭).

5.

6. G♯ or A♭.

7. Melody: Passage 1ii melody is in the horns (Passage 1i was in the trumpets), and now an octave lower. Accompaniment: Passage 1i had a harpsichord figure/riff in semiquavers, filling in the gaps between phrases. Passage 1ii has a countermelody, higher than the melody, in flutes/piccolo. The bass and percussion are similar in both passages.

8. Trombone or tuba.

9.

10.

11. (a) Imitation.

    (b) Pedal or ostinato/riff.

    (c) Antiphony.

68 Answers

Test 2

1. (a) Glissando.

   (b) Glockenspiel.

2. Bar 5: I (F); bar 6¹: IV (B♭); bar 6³: V⁷d (C/B♭); bar 7³: VI (Dm).

3.

4. (a) Bar 13: G major.

   (b) Bar 17: E major.

5. Tonic pedal.

   > A pedal is usually either a tonic pedal or a dominant pedal.

6. Polyphonic/contrapuntal or imitative.

7. A trill.

8. Passage 1iii is the almost the same as Passage 1i; both have an AAB shape. Passage 1i has an introduction (four bars long). Passage 1iii has a shorter introduction (two bars) and a coda/end section consisting of four bars of new material. Passage 1ii has no introduction, and the A melody appears once only. The A section is extended by adding the contrapuntal section (this could be described as AC).

9. A decorated perfect cadence. The melody has a descending scale of E major, harmonised in 6ths by the inner parts. The bass is an ascending scale, partly chromatic. The two scales are in contrary motion. The violins play pizzicato/plucked. Double stopping is used on the final chord.

10.

Test 3

1. ABA, or ternary.

2.

3. (a) Bar 3: F minor (or f – in lower case).

   (b) Bar 19: E♭ minor.

4.

5. There is more quaver movement in the melody. The bass plays crotchets on beats 2 and 4, syncopated rhythm. The rhythm of the opening section (rhythmic motif from bar 1, repeated quavers) stops.

6. (a) Trumpet.

   (b) It is muted, with a mute.

   (c) Piano (or vibraphone).

7. Triple time, three beats in a bar, waltz rhythm, faster. The melody is decorated with an anacrusis (bar 54) syncopated upbeat (bar 62). Chromatic and auxiliary notes are added (bars 56–57). Leaps of a 5th (bar 12) filled in with smaller intervals (bar 74). Semiquaver decoration (bar 78). An elaborate, virtuoso fill between phrases (bars 68–70). The long final note in (bar 17) is replaced by a new dotted crotchet/three quavers figure lasting four bars (bars 83–86).

   > Make your points concisely without writing long sentences. Use small handwriting or bullet points if it helps you to get six different features in.

8. Perfect cadence.

9. (a) Bar 80 beat 2.

   (b) Bar 72 beat 2 or bar 80 beat 2.

   (c) Bar 75.

10. Bars 67–70.

11.

Test 4

1.

2. Introduction with ABAA¹ melody, each section is four bars in length. A final section/coda of eight bars is added to make the overall shape: Intro + ABAA¹C. The melody is made up of two-bar phrases.

   > Try to make letter descriptions of structure as simple as possible. Decide whether you are discussing groups of two-bar phrases or four-bar phrases. Here ABAA¹ based on four-bar sections is clearer than AABBAAA¹A¹ using two-bar phrases. Adding a short description of the length of phrases/sections makes your thinking clear to the examiner.

3.

Instrumentation and texture in bars 5–8	Changes in bars 9–10
Trombone melody	Melody in violins/strings
Countermelody/answering fanfare in trumpets	Smoother/legato
	Brass/woodwind countermelody
Repeated rhythm in snare drum	Bass sustained not detached
Tuba/double bass alternating tonic-dominant	

4.

5. Dominant pedal (E). Dissonance/clash of chords against the pedal. Avoids perfect cadence/interrupted cadence/modulation away from the tonic. Effect of suspense, suggesting that the music is continuing.

6. Uses the motif from the first bar of the melody only. Shorter/played twice only.

7. (a) a trill.

   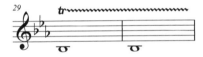

   (b) tremolo.

8. (a) (French) horns.

   (b) Trumpets.

9. Syncopated rhythm/irregular grouping of quavers into 3+3+2. Pizzicato/plucking in cellos/double bass. Xylophone. Dissonance/minor 2nds. Using ideas first heard at the end of phrases (bars 34–35 and 37–38). Descending semiquaver figure in bass/bass clarinet. Melodic interest is passed between different instruments.

Test 5

1.

2. Both sections have the melody in the violins, playing in octaves. Both use an accompanying chordal riff, played by brass (horns and trumpets) in bars 6–18 and woodwind (flutes and clarinets) in bars 20–32. Snare drum rhythm throughout. Syncopated bass/tuba.

3. (a)

   (b) (i) bar 17³–18¹: perfect. (ii) bar 31³–32¹: interrupted

4. Bar 22: IV (A♭); bar 26: II (Fm); bar 27: V⁷ (B♭⁷); bar 28: I (E♭).

5. Tambourine.

6.

7. AAB structure in bars 6–18. The A sections are each four bars long, but the B section is longer. In Passage 1ii the B section is shorter (2 bars), using the two-note motif which is characteristic of the theme.

8. (a) Strumming.

   (b) Glissando.

9. Xylophone.

10. New rhythmic material/changing time signatures in the introduction. Final section/coda uses repeated motif from introduction to Passage 1i. Countermelody in horns.

Prescribed Orchestral Scores

Test 1

1. (a) Trill.

   (b) Acciaccatura.

   (c) Appoggiatura.

2. (a) B minor.

   (b) A minor.

3. 'Solo' indicates only one instrumentalist should play. 'Tutti' means 'all' parts in an ensemble play together.

4. The solo bassoon is accompanied by the continuo only: a solo cello bass line with a keyboard instrument to fill in the texture. Bars 1–4: detached chords on the last note of the descending scale figure extended into a cadence figure in quavers. Bar 5: demisemiquaver passagework sequence accompanied by detached quavers. Bars 6–8: return of regular quaver movement in the continuo, outlining tonic-dominant chords as the key changes. Bars 9–10¹:

solo demisemiquavers accompanied by detached quavers (repeated E/dominant to prepare perfect cadence in A minor).

5. Pitch: 1A is at a lower pitch, about a tone lower than 1B.

   Timbre: 1A uses period instruments compared to the modern instruments in 1B. The bassoon tone in 1A is 'woodier' and quieter compared to the clear, stronger sound of the modern bassoon in 1B. The cello in 1B uses more vibrato. The harpsichord sounds stronger in 1A; the tone is harsher, compared to the soft, bright sound of 1B. The 1B harpsichord is also placed in the background of the recording; in 1A the harpsichord is more forward, having equal prominence with the bassoon and cello.

   Ornamentation: The soloist in 1A plays the notes as written. The 1B soloist elaborates the melody, adding ornamentation or decoration: e.g. the decoration to the descending scale at bar 2; using demisemiquavers to fill leaps (bars 3^3, 4^1 and 7); the added trill at bar 7; an extra passing note between C and E at bar 10.

   The realisation of the continuo: Both harpsichord players improvise chords, following the rhythm of the bass part. The player in 1A has a more varied approach: detached quavers at bars 5 and 9 are staccato, left hand only, without filled-in chords; bars 7–8 use spread chords and added notes/rhythms to decorate the harmony.

   Further observations: 1A is slower than 1B. The solo bassoon is more dominant in 1B; the instruments are more equally balanced in 1A.

   > The bar numbers help to show that you have listened in detail.

6. (a) This extract is the second solo or episode. The movement is in ritornello form.

   (b) Descending scale figure and rhythm derived from the opening motif of the B material in the opening ritornello, first heard on unison violins (bars 5–6).

Test 2

1. Repeated demisemiquaver broken-chord figure, outlining chords of E minor, A minor, B major; followed by a statement of the opening ritornello theme.

2. (a) (Descending) sequence.

   (b) IVb; A minor, first inversion.

   (c) Appoggiatura.

   (d) Double/triple stopping.

3. [musical notation: bars 13–16]

4. Melody in 2nd violins. 1st violins have the accompaniment: demisemiquaver broken chords; arpeggiando technique; repeated bowing across the strings; bowing marked as slurred 3+1. Lower strings play repeated quavers. Melody ends with E minor chord (bar 15^1) in full strings, followed by a tutti silence. Contrasting texture and thematic material at the end of the tutti (bars 15–16^1): descending scale figure in octaves.

5. Extract begins in E minor, the tonic key of the movement. It modulates to the dominant minor, B minor. The second solo then continues in the new dominant key.

6. The interpretation of the bassoon solo: In bars 1–2 the articulation in 2A is clearer; the bassoonist in 2B plays the broken-chord figure more smoothly. The Lombardic (Scotch snap) rhythms in bar 4 are firmer in 2A, gentler in 2B. In 2A the A♯ at bar 8^3 is played as a crotchet, with the D and C♯ at the end of the bar altered to semiquavers; 2B plays the rhythm as printed. 2B has a slight ritardando at bar 9, before the chromatic passage over the held E in the bass at bar 9^3. 2B adds a trill on the B at bar 7. The trills in 2B are more elaborate: at bar 5 the first (upper) note of the trill is sustained to emphasise the appoggiatura/suspension; the trill in 2B at bar 8^1 is longer than the mordent used in 2A; a turn is added in 2B at the end of the trill at bar 11^2.

   Period and modern performance: 2A is performed on modern instruments; 2B on period instruments, using a smaller orchestra – one violin to a part from bar 13. The violin demisemiquaver figures (bars 2–4) are quieter in 2B. The 2A strings make more use of vibrato; in 2B shorter bows make long notes less sustained. 2A is at modern pitch: it sounds about a tone higher than 2B, which is at the lower pitch used in Vivaldi's time. 2A's modern bassoon has a brighter tone than the softer tone of the bassoon in 2B.

   The role of the harpsichord: The 2A harpsichord is quieter and busier; 2B adds fewer melodic decorations. At the beginning of the extract 2A plays chords on the crotchet beats, while 2B plays chords on beats 1 and 3. The 2A harpsichord improvises demisemiquaver broken-chord figures at bars 3^1, 4^1, 5^3 and 6^3 in response to the bassoon and violins. At bar 9^3 2A plays a spread chord over the held E, but 2B has no right-hand chord, leaving the texture bare.

The balance of the recording: Both are modern recordings. The orchestra in 2A sounds slightly further back compared to the closer mic sound in 2B. In 2B the solo bassoon is recorded quite close compared to the 2A bassoon, which sounds more distant. The harpsichord is placed in the background in 2A, difficult to hear at times; in 2B the harpsichord is more prominent, with improvised detail easy to distinguish (e.g. bar 11³). The bass in 2B is stronger, with the left hand of the harpsichord very distinct.

> You are not expected to include all of these points! Aim to make a number of comparisons and provide bar references for examples.

Test 3

1. D♭ major.

2. (a) Both bassoons play the printed part.
   (b) Pause.

3. The strings play repeated homophonic crotchets to accompany the melody, which is passed between 1st violins and the cellos and double basses. The woodwind play sustained notes, beginning with a solo bassoon countermelody in a high register and followed by homophonic chords (excluding flute) to build the texture. The sustained melody in the 1st violins at bar 25 is doubled by solo oboe.

4.

5. Tempo: Extract 3A is slower than Extract 3B. 3A has a ritardando (slowing down) in the last two bars (bars 46–47); 3B maintains the fast tempo to the end of the extract. The final chord is more sustained in 3A; it is cut off more dramatically in 3B.

   Balance: The balance between the instruments is similar in the two performances. The solo oboe part in 3A can be heard more clearly.

   Articulation: There is more variety in articulation in 3A. The final note of the opening melody is more staccato (1st violins in bar 7, cellos and basses in bar 11). Both performances play the repeated crotchets staccato, however in bars 21–24 of 3A the crotchets are more sustained (legato). 3B is more forceful in the full orchestra passage from bar 31, with shorter, more staccato repeated notes.

   Further observations: 3B is at a lower pitch than 3A (about a semitone lower), which indicates a period performance; 3A uses modern instruments. The quality of the recordings is similar, both modern recordings in quite a resonant acoustic (heard in the dying away of the sound of the final chords).

> The bullet points in the question give you some guidance, but comment on other differences if you hear them.

6. Submediant key; G major chord; distant from the tonic.

7. Return of the main theme, in E♭ major (tonic key). Horns accompany. Leads to full orchestra, imitative texture.

8. This extract is the end of the development (or episode, section C), before the recapitulation. The movement is in sonata rondo form. Theme is in its second subject form.

Test 4

1. (a) (i) Both horns play the printed part.
   (ii) Forzando, a sudden accent.
   (b) Repeated quavers.

2.

3. Polyphonic texture at the beginning. Full orchestra in bars 1–4, including horns, trumpets and timpani. Counterpoint made up of two themes: 'horn call' theme in upper parts (flute, oboes, brass, violins); main theme in bass parts (violas, cellos, clarinets, bassoons). Melody in upper parts extended into long notes, with suspensions in 2nd violins and 1st clarinet at bars 7–8. Main theme repeated at bar 4 (with double basses added); extended into ascending scale, reaching F at bar 10. Dominant/F pedal (dominant of B♭ major) from bar 10 in: cellos and basses (repeated crotchets); bassoons (sustained note for eight bars); antiphonal exchange of four repeated notes in horns and trumpets (an octave apart).

> Name instruments and describe how they combine with others. Avoid general descriptions of texture such as 'thick' and 'thin'.

4. Key of B♭ major. Alternates tonic (I) and dominant 7th (V⁷) chords. Repeated use of suspension on B♭ (resolving to A).

5. Pitch: 4A is at a slightly lower pitch than 4B. 4A is a period performance, using instrument and performance practices of Haydn's time, when pitch would have been lower than the standard concert pitch today.

   Balance of instrumental parts: In 4A trumpets and drums strengthen the impact of the opening tutti; trumpets and drums are not included in 4B. As a result it is easier to hear the main theme in 4B. The violins are clearly heard in both performances, but the contrapuntal entries in other parts are clearer in 4B, for example the cellos and basses at bar 4 and the oboes at bar 9. The antiphonal descending scales in the violins from bar 19 are more equally balanced in 4B.

Dynamics: The opening of the extract is louder in 4A. Both performances have similar dynamics. In 4B there is a slight diminuendo followed by a crescendo towards the fortissimo at bar 29; 4A is more consistently loud.

Further observations: 4A is slightly faster than 4B. Both performances use staccato as marked, but in bars 5–6 the violins in 4A play legato while the 4B violins are detached. In the strings longer notes are more sustained in 4B; in 4A the shorter bows used in period performance make long notes less sustained. 4B is recorded in a more resonant acoustic.

6. This extract is from the exposition, end of the first-subject section of sonata-rondo form.

Test 5

1. (a) Sweetly.

   (b) Sforzando, a sudden accent.

   (c) A little crescendo, getting louder very gradually.

2.

3. Begins in A major (dominant key of D major, the concerto's tonic key), using chords I (A) and V (E). Dominant pedal trill in violin in bars 1–5. Repeat of melody in A minor in bars 10–23. After the diatonic harmonies of bars 1–23, bars 24–29 use a chromatic chord – the diminished 7th (bars 24, 26, 28, 29), which changes the mood. The extract ends with chords Ic and V⁷ (a perfect cadence in A major if the extract continued).

4. Elaborate, virtuoso solo. Fast moving, mostly in semiquavers. Ascending arpeggios or broken-chord figures in bars 30–33; descending arpeggios in bars 34–35. Wide range, covering two and a half octaves. Melody outlined by the highest note of the arpeggios (doubled by the violins). Use of turns to decorate the arpeggio in bar 31.

5. Tempo: The woodwind melody is slightly faster in 5A. Both performances slow for the violin melody at bars 6–8 (5B is slower than 5A here) and for the *dolce* repeated A♯ at bars 24 and 26. 5A is more consistent in tempo. 5B uses rubato for the triplets at bars 25 and 27. The semiquavers and the arpeggios at the end are faster in 5B (from bar 28); 5A has a slight ritardando (slowing down) on the final arpeggio (bar 35).

The solo violin part: 5A has a consistent tone and vibrato throughout the extract. 5B is similar, but there are differences in bowing and articulation in places, e.g. in the triplets at bars 9–23. 5B uses a portamento (a slide) between B and E at bar 8 and a harmonic on the A at bar 9¹.

The overall sound of each recording: 5A has better recorded sound, a modern recording. The hiss in 5B and the thinner sound of woodwind and violins suggests an older recording (from the 1930s). In 5A the balance between solo and orchestra is more equal; the melody in the first violins from bar 10 is heard more clearly. In 5B the solo violin sounds more forward and the orchestra more distant.

Further observations: The violins in the orchestra in 5B make much more use of portamento (expressive slides between the notes), for example the intervals of a 5th and 4th (descending) at bars 13 and 15 respectively and a 4th at bar 18 (ascending), but also when the melody is moving in steps of a tone or semitone.

6. (a) This extract is part of the solo exposition or the first solo. This is the second subject, before the development. The overall structure is sonata form.

   (b) Solo violin has an ascending scale theme in split octaves. Leads to violin semiquavers, accompanied by woodwind antiphony with strings, E major and A minor chords. Unaccompanied solo violin for four bars decorating the note E on semiquavers, slowing to triplets.

Test 6

1. (a) A strong accent followed by a sudden piano (soft).

   (b) Both performers play the printed part.

   (c) Always very loud.

2. Trill, sustained throughout bars 1–12. Begins on E for six bars; changes from trill on F♯ (bars 1–4) to trill using F♮ (bars 5–6). Ascending chromatically in minims in bars 7–8, ending with a four-bar trill on A (bars 9–12).

3.

4. Dramatic entry of the full orchestra, **ff** at bar 19. Unexpected chord of B♭ major (the flattened submediant); interrupted cadence. Short phrases, separated by tutti silences. Repeated semiquavers in strings and timpani. D⁷ chord in first inversion at bar 22¹. *Sforzandi* accents on second and fourth beats in bars 26–29. Antiphonal exchanges between upper strings and full orchestra. Strings in octaves. Repeat of semiquaver motif in ascending pattern (bars 30–31).

Final D major chord in second inversion at bar 32; full orchestra pause for solo cadenza.

> It is important to comment on both the orchestra and tonality and harmony. You may lose marks if you only answer on the aspect that you find easier to answer.

5. The orchestra in the two performances: 6A uses a larger orchestra, with more stringed instruments, which gives more weight to the accents in the tutti section. The timpani in 6B plays with harder sticks: the roll at bar 32 is 'rounded off' to make a more distinct end.

   Dynamics and expression: The *pp* passage at the beginning is quieter in 6B; in 6A the detached quavers are clearer, very staccato. 6B has a slight slowing down (ritardando) in the oboes/horns motif at bar 11. The *sforzandi* accents are observed by both performances, but the larger orchestra in 6A accents each crotchet beat strongly; 6B is lighter with the first and third beats. 6A plays a longer crotchet at bar 22^1 than 6B. Both performances slow down in bar 31, but 6A has a slightly broader ritardando here.

   The interpretation of the solo part: The trills in 6A are played at a more even speed; the soloist in 6B emphasises changes of pitch (e.g. the G at bar 8^1 and the A at bar 9^1) by lengthening the first note and beginning the trill more slowly. 6B uses more rubato (expressive variation of tempo) in the scales at bars 13–18, for example making the note A longer each time in bars 13–14. 6A plays the scales in a stricter tempo.

   The quality of the recorded sound: Both are modern recordings. 6A is recorded in a more resonant acoustic, as you can hear in the silences in bars 20 and 22.

   Further observation: In bar 17 the violas play a C♯ in 6A but an A (as printed in the score) in 6B.

6. It represents the point at which the soloist plays an improvised cadenza; the cadenza section will usually end with a trill, as notated in bar 32^3.

Jazz works June 2011–January 2013

Test 1

1. Contrapuntal, interweaving melodic lines (trumpet, clarinet, trombone) – New Orleans polyphony. Rhythm-section accompaniment: piano chords/comping, bass (tuba) alternating tonic and dominant notes.

2. First chorus has a clarinet solo. Trumpet and trombone do not play.

3.
Instrument	Prominent features of the music played
Trumpet	Swung rhythm/dotted notes
Clarinet	Fast vibrato, descending arpeggio figuration, wide range, glissandi/slides, swung rhythm/dotted notes
Trombone	Glissando, held notes/minims

4. (a) Johnny Dodds.

   (b) 1927.

5. Four bars, linking/modulating to the next section; the whole ensemble plays, followed by a trumpet solo.

Test 2

1. Louis Armstrong.

2. Piano and banjo: chords/comping. Tuba: detached/staccato crotchets, first and third beats. Cymbal: second and fourth beats, sound choked off with hand.

3. (a) Four phrases, two sections AB (complete melody is three sections, ABA). A section: opening phrase is repeated, with varied repeat of chromatic figure. Major key (C major), second phrase altered to finish in the tonic key. B section: broken chord/arpeggio figure. Contrasting use of minor key/chord of E minor. Ascending scale to repeat of phrase in higher key. Gradual ascent of melody to final high note.

   (b) Rip/glissando/wide vibrato.

4. Trumpet solo continues. Return of opening/A phrase. Higher register, wider range. More virtuosic, wide leaps, solo ends with unaccompanied break.

5. Chicago.

Test 3

1. Very fast, irregular and varied lengths of phrases, dissonant notes or notes fitting in with complex harmonies, repetition or combination of motifs/phrases/licks favoured by the player.

2. Max Roach.

3. Sequence (repetition of a melodic phrase a tone lower). The chords/harmony move through the circle of 5ths.

4. The bass plays in a high register, the bass drum is more prominent, and there are more interjections from the drums.

5. The dominant note/F is held in the saxophone – prepares for the return to the tonic – echoed an octave lower by the piano. The bass drum plays three notes – usually it plays only single notes. The texture is more sparse, with the longer notes providing a contrast from the constant quaver movement of the rest of the chorus.

6. The alto saxophone solo continues into Chorus 2. Quotation from clarinet solo, *High Society*. The bass starts off this chorus in a higher register.

Test 4

1. (a) Dizzy Gillespie.

    (b) Alto saxophone.

2. Fast, crotchet rhythm, syncopated/off-beat accents e.g. on bass drum. No cymbal. Drops out for final alto saxophone/trumpet phrase.

3. (a) Octave.

    (b) Very fast, virtuosic, bebop-style melody. Four sections/phrases. First phrase: played in unison. Second phrase: trumpet solo, constant quaver movement. Third phrase: alto saxophone melody more fragmented, broken up by rests, longer notes. Fourth phrase: starts as a duet in 3rds, descending octave leap, in octaves to finish.

4. (a) Alto saxophone solo, two solo choruses. Cymbal, double bass and piano added. Walking bass. Based on chords/changes from *Cherokee*.

    (b) Coda/at the end.

5. New York.

Test 5

1. (a) Gil Evans.

    (b) Paul Chambers.

2. Swing/dotted rhythm on the ride cymbal to keep the time. A rimshot on the fourth beat of each bar. A single note on cymbal on the first beat of a chorus. Bass drum reinforces staccato/cut off half way through brass scale in B chorus. A fill at the end leads into the next chorus.

3. (a) (French) horns.

    (b) Beginning of Chorus A1/first chorus, after the slow introduction.

4. He exploits the middle range of the instrument. Limited vibrato or colouring of the tone. A narrow range of notes at the beginning of the solo. Short phrases separated by silences.

5. (a) Brass chords, in close harmony. Ascending scale, legato/smooth, in minims, with one abrupt staccato break (accented by the bass drum). Walking bass, four beats in a bar, moving in a sequence of 4ths and 5ths. Dissonant 'hit' chord for full band at the end.

    (b) Saxophones more prominent in B1, B2 is more brass dominated. The rhythm of B1 is syncopated/irregular lengths of notes, B2 is in even minims.

6. Solo continues, with accompanying horn riffs, and a suddenly accented drum note.

Test 6

1. (a) Pizzicato/plucked.

    (b) Drums: repeated swung rhythm on the ride cymbal, drum rimshot on the fourth beat of the bar. Bass: walking bass, regular crotchet pulse.

    (c) Jimmy Cobb.

2. Riff/ostinato. Chordal/triadic. Staccato, detached chords separated by rests. Outlines one chord (Gm^7). Syncopated, anticipates the beat.

3. (Answer refers to 4 sections: A1, A2, A3, A4.) A1: Trumpet begins with short phrases, then a longer phrase with double time; accompanied by the staccato riff. A2: Sustained notes in the trumpet; the riff becomes smooth/legato, varied and extended; trumpet uses the same legato phrasing as the riff. A3: Trumpet dissonant leap (augmented 4th/diminished 5th), cymbal splash response to change of mood; high register in trumpet, descending phrase, followed by double-bass ascending scale to high register. A4: Trumpet focus on narrow range of pitch, ending on repeated note; diminuendo/getting quieter to the end in both melody and accompaniment; bass and cymbal finish off the piece.

4. No B/bridge section; this chorus is AAAA, choruses 1–3 are AABA.

5. New York.

Jazz works June 2013–January 2015

Test 1

1. (a) Lil Hardin/Lil Armstrong.

    (b) Tonic-dominant octaves in the left hand. Syncopated rhythm.

2. (a) Trombone.

    (b) Glissando; fall-off.

3. Trombone solo accompanied by piano/banjo comping. Break for solo trumpet. Trumpet solo melody, joined by countermelodies in clarinet and trombone. Stop time: solo trumpet accompanied by detached chords in ensemble. Typical polyphonic texture of New Orleans jazz; collective improvisation.

4. Leads to final coda. Duet between guitar and trumpet: trading phrases; antiphonal exchanges (not imitation). Diminished chord in guitar creates an inconclusive ending.

Test 2

1. Piano, banjo.
2. 32-bar structure. Two-bar break in the middle and end. Very static harmony (chord I and V) in the first half; faster harmonic movement in second half.
3. Swung quavers, syncopation. First half comprises four phrases. Similar rhythm for each phrase, e.g. syncopated two-note upbeat/anacrusis. Gradual ascent of first note of each phrase. Break at end of first half. Rip/glissando to highest note of melody (B♭). Second half more virtuosic: broken chord/arpeggio figures; chromatic triplets; wider range; ends in high register. Sustained high G with shake/lip trill.
4. (a) First chorus. After the introduction.

    (b) Clarinet solo. High register, smear/glissando. Piano and banjo accompaniment continues.
5. (a) Chicago.

    (b) OKeh.

Test 3

1. (a) Trombone.

    (b) Plunger mute, with a second mute fixed inside the instrument to create a buzzing sound. Vocalisation to create the 'ya-ya' effect.
2. Saxophone riff in unison. Syncopated chords on brass (trumpets and trombone), alternating open and closed plunger mute. Pizzicato double bass plays a walking bass. Strummed chords on guitar. Drums. Occasional offbeat chords on piano.
3. Double bass begins (in the second chorus) with an ascending scale (previously a repeated descending figure). The solo is higher in pitch, with less use of the vocalised ya-ya effect. There are more syncopated piano chords towards the end of the chorus.
4. Piano solo featuring ascending and descending scales in whole tones and dissonant chords. Saxophone riff is now in one-bar units (previously repeated every two bars).
5. 1940.

Test 4

1. (a) Solo break, call and response with full band. Part of the rhythm section, walking bass, four beats in a bar.

    (b) Pizzicato/plucked.

    (c) Jimmy Blanton.
2. First chorus: Use of four-note cell ('x' motif) in three groups of instruments – saxophones, trombones, trumpets. Chordal arrangement of motif. Final note of motif sustained to form full chord. Clarinet has the highest note of the chord. Second chorus: Sustained, loud chord in full brass (trumpets and trombones) plus high clarinet. Dissonant chord, use of interval of 4ths. Melody in unison saxophones (two altos, one tenor, one baritone). Reference to whole tone, augmented 4th, outlining chord of E♭m⁹.
3. (a) 12-bar blues.

    (b) Minor key (E♭ minor). Aeolian mode.

    (c) Last two choruses (Choruses 6 and 7). Before the coda.
4. Chicago.

Test 5

1. John Lewis.
2. Melody in the right hand; syncopated; opens with repeated leaps of a 5th. Rests/silences between phrases. Melody begins in a high register; ends in a low register.
3. Full band, but no piano. Melody in trumpet, doubled an octave below by the baritone saxophone. Chordal texture, harmony in parallel chords – rich, dissonant sounds of 9ths, 11ths. Tuba plays the bass of the chords. Double bass, pizzicato, playing a walking bass.
4. (a) At the beginning; Chorus 1; the A section of the AABA theme.

    (b) An extra bar extends the final phrase: the ascending 3rds figure is now over two bars instead of one. Final three chords are a repeat of the first three chords of the theme, using longer note values (augmentation). Additional accents and syncopations on the drums and cymbals. Final chord has a tuba tremolo and a drum fill.

Test 6

1. Nine.
2. Double bass, plucked/pizzicato, walking bass, steady crotchet beat. Drums, played on brushes. Piano, enters half way through extract, detached chords, complex chords (9ths, 7ths).
3. (a) Beginning: Trumpet melody accompanied by sustained chords in brass/saxophones. Variety of textures – chordal/close harmony, unison, octaves. End: Syncopated chords, improvised trumpet melody. Fall-off on final band chord. Rest of solo accompanied by rhythm section only.

    (b) Any two of: middle range, limited vibrato, economy of style/use of silences, very little use of double time.
4. End of Chorus 2 and beginning of Chorus 3. Overall structure is three choruses, AABA, 32-bar song form.
5. New York.

Track Information by Question

Instrumental Repertoire 1700–1830

Introduction

Tracks 1–2
Mozart: Symphony No. 39 in E♭, K. 543 (Menuetto allegretto)
Capella Istropolitana, Barry Wordsworth (cond)
Mozart Symphonies Nos. 34, 35 and 39
Naxos 8.550186, Track 10, 1:53–2:14, 2:14–2:35

Tracks 3–7
Mozart: *Ah, vous dirai-je, maman*, K. 265
Jenö Jandó (piano)
Mozart: Piano Sonatas Nos. 11 and 14
Naxos 8.550258, Track 8
0:00–0:48, 0:49–1:31, 3:45–4:30, 4:30–5:11, 5:54–6:52

Track 8
Handel: Suite No. 7 in G minor (*Passacaille*)
Alan Cuckston (harpsichord)
Harpsichord Suites Nos. 6–8
Naxos 8.550416, Track 10 complete

Tracks 9–10
Bach: Brandenburg Concerto No. 4 (mvt 2)
Cologne Chamber Orchestra, Helmut Muller-Bruhl (cond)
Bach Brandenburg Concertos, Vol. 2
Naxos 8.554608, Track 2, 0:00–0:45, 2:41–2:57

Tracks 11–14
Beethoven: Symphony No. 6 'Pastoral' (mvt 1)
Nicholaus Esterhazy Sinfonia, Belas Drahos (cond)
Symphonies Nos. 1 and 6
Naxos 8.553474, Track 5
0:00–0:06, 0:55–1:05, 4:53–5:38, 9:20–9:26

Tests 1–6

Test 1: Track 15
Beethoven: Clarinet Trio Op. 38 (Andante con variazioni)
Jürgen Demmler (clarinet), Markus Tillier (cello), Peter Grabinger (piano)
Beethoven/Ries: Clarinet Trios
Naxos 8.553389, Track 8, 0:00–1:56 and 2:50–3:17

Test 1: Track 16
Beethoven: Septet in E♭ major, Op. 20 (*Tema con variazioni: andante*)
Chamber Music for Horns, Wind and Strings
Naxos 8.553090, Track 4, 0:00–1:59 and 3:08–3:42

Test 2: Track 17
Mozart: Symphony No. 40 (Molto allegro)
Capella Istropolitana, Barry Wordsworth (cond)
Mozart Symphonies Nos. 40 and 41
Naxos 8.550299, Track 1, 0:00–0:47, 3:45–4:25 and 6:33–6:57

Test 3: Track 18
Haydn: Quartet No. 27 in D major, Op. 20, No. 4 (Un poco adagio e affettuoso)
Kodály Quartet
Haydn String Quartets Op. 20 'Sun' Nos. 4–6
Naxos 8.550702, Track 2, 0:30–1:36, 2:42–3:43 and 5:22–5:47

Test 4: Track 19
Paganini: Caprice No. 24 in A minor
Ilya Kaler (violin)
24 Caprices, Op.1
Naxos 8.550717, Track 24, 0:00–1:40, 1:59–2:21 and 2:40–3:17

Test 5: Track 20
Schubert: Octet (Theme and Variations)
The Gaudier Ensemble
Schubert Octet
Hyperion CDA67339, Track 4, 0:00–1:09, 3:21–4:40 and 7:08–8:14

Test 6: Track 21
Bach: Brandenburg Concerto No.1 (mvt 3)
Cologne Chamber Orchestra, Helmut Muller-Bruhl (cond)
Bach Brandenburg Concertos Vol. 1
Naxos 8.554607, Track 3, 0:00–0:28, 1:11–2:07 and 2:40–3:04

Popular Instrumental Music 1900–Present Day

Tests 1–5

Test 1: Track 22
Morton Stevens: *Hawaii Five-O*
Philharmonic Concert Orchestra
100 Greatest TV Themes
Silva Screen Records, TVPMCD807
Disc 2 track 7, 0:00–0:29, 0:29–0:51, 2:45–3:18

Test 2: Track 23
Henry Mancini: *Newhart*
Daniel Caine Orchestra
100 Greatest TV Themes
Silva Screen Records, TVPMCD605
Disc 3 track 11, 0:00–0:41, 1:08–1:32, 1:33–2:19

Test 3: Track 24
John Barry: *A Man Alone* and *Alone in Three-Quarter Time* from The Ipcress File
The Ipcress File: original soundtrack
Silva Screen Records, FILMCD606
Track 5, 1:09–2:35 and track 3, 0:00–0:59

Test 4: Track 25
Barry Gray: *Thunderbirds Are Go!* and *Lady Penelope on the move*
Thunderbirds original soundtrack
Silva Screen Records, FILMCD606
Track 5, 3:30–4:25 and track 13, 0:26–0:55

Test 5: Track 26
Elmer Bernstein: *The Magnificent Seven*
The Essential Elmer Bernstein Film Music Collection
Silva Screen Records, SILCD1178
Track 1, 0:00–0:48, 1:15–1:34, 4:10–4:48

Prescribed Orchestral Scores

Test 1 Extract 1A: Track 27
Vivaldi: Bassoon Concerto in E minor, RV484 (mvt 1)
Milan Turkovic (bassoon), The English Concert, Trevor Pinnock (harpsichord)
Vivaldi Flute Concertos
Classic FM CFMFW137, Track 28, 1:56–2:40

Test 1 Extract 1B: Track 28
Vivaldi: Bassoon Concerto in E minor, RV484 (mvt 1)
Klaus Thunemann (bassoon), I Musici
Vivaldi Bassoon Concertos
Universal Classics (Phillips), CD 2 Track 13, 1:39–2:17

Test 2 Extract 2A: Track 29
Vivaldi: Bassoon Concerto in E minor, RV484 (mvt 1)
František Hermann (bassoon), Capella Istropolitana, Jaroslav Krček (conductor)
The Best of Vivaldi
Naxos 8.556655, Track 23, 0:46–1:42

Test 2 Extract 2B: Track 30
Vivaldi: Bassoon Concerto in E minor, RV484 (mvt 1)
Frans Robert Berkhout (bassoon), Suave Melodia
Vivaldi: Concerti & Cantata with Bassoon
Etcetera KTC1324, Track 14, 0:47–1:47

Test 3 Extract 3A: Track 31
Haydn: Symphony No. 103 in E♭ major (mvt 4)
Orchestra della Svizzera Italiana, Howard Shelley (conductor)
Haydn: The London Symphonies
Hyperion CDS44371/4, CD 4 Track 8, 3:01–3:42

Test 3 Extract 3B: Track 32
Haydn: Symphony No. 103 in E♭ major (mvt 4)
Les Musiciens du Louvre-Grenobles, Marc Minkowski (conductor)
Haydn: 12 London Symphonies
Naïve V5176, CD 4 Track 8, 2:42–3:18

Test 4 Extract 4A: Track 33
Haydn: Symphony No. 103 in E♭ major (mvt 4)
Orchestra of the 18th century, Frans Brüggen (conductor)
Haydn: The 'London' Symphonies Vol. 1
Universal Classics (Phillips), CD 1 Track 12, 0:57–1:25

Test 4 Extract 4B: Track 34
Haydn: Symphony No. 103 in E♭ major (mvt 4)
London Philharmonic Orchestra, Eugen Jochum (conductor)
Haydn Symphonies 103 & 104, Brahms Haydn Variations
Deutsche Grammophon, Track 4, 1:01–1:29

Test 5 Extract 5A: Track 35
Beethoven: Violin Concerto in D, Op. 61 (mvt 1)
Herman Krebbers (violin), Royal Concertgebuow Orchestra, Bernard Haitink (conductor)
Beethoven: Complete Concertos Vol. 2
Universal Classics (Phillips), CD 2 Track 1, 5:14–6:36

Test 5 Extract 5B: Track 36
Beethoven: Violin Concerto in D, Op. 61 (mvt 1)
Joseph Szigeti (violin), British Symphony Orchestra, Bruno Walter (conductor)
Great Violinists: Szigeti – Beethoven/Mozart Violin Concertos
Naxos 8.110946, Track 4, 4:50–6:11

Test 6 Extract 6A: Track 37
Beethoven: Violin Concerto in D, Op. 61 (mvt 1)
Henryk Szeryng (violin), Royal Concertgebuow Orchestra, Bernard Haitinik (conductor)
Beethoven Violin Concerto
Classic FM CFMFW075, Track 1, 19:19–20:32

Test 6 Extract 6B: Track 38
Beethoven: Violin Concerto in D, Op. 61 (mvt 1)
Joshua Bell (violin), Camerata Salzburg, Sir Roger Norrington (conductor)
Mendelssohn/Beethoven Violin Concertos
Sony, Track 4, 17:54–19:06

Jazz 1920–1960

Prescribed works June 2011–Jan 2013
Tests 1–2: Tracks 39–40
Louis Armstrong: *Alligator Crawl*
Louis Armstrong: 25 Greatest Hot Fives & Hot Sevens
Living Era AJA5171, Track 9, 0:30–0:59 and 1:08–1:46

Tests 3–4: Tracks 41–42
Charlie Parker: *Ko-Ko*
Ornithology: Classic Recordings (1945–1947)
Naxos 8.120571, Track 3, 0:25–1:15 and 0:00–0:24

Tests 5–6: Tracks 43–44
Miles Davis: *It Ain't Necessarily So*
Porgy and Bess
Sony Jazz CK65141, Track 10, 1:31–2:14 and 3:24–4:24

Prescribed works June 2013–Jan 2015

Tests 1–2: Tracks 45–46
Louis Armstrong: *Hotter Than That*
Louis Armstrong: 25 Greatest Hot Fives & Hot Sevens
Living Era AJA5171, Track 16, 2:14–2:52 and 0:09–0:43

Tests 3–4: Tracks 47–48
Duke Ellington: *Koko*
Cotton Tail: Classic Recordings, Vol. 7 (1940)
Naxos 8.120738, Track 3, 0:32–1:08 and 1:44–2:22

Tests 5–6: Tracks 49–50
Miles Davis: *Boplicity*
Birth of the Cool (Rudy Van Gelder edition)
Capitol Jazz/Blue Note Records, Track 8, 2:26–2:59 and
1:35–2:26

Glossary

Acciaccatura. A very short ornamental note played just before a principal melodic note.

Aeolian mode. A scale that uses the following pattern of tones (T) and semitones (s): T–s–T–T–s–T–T. When starting on A, it consists of all the white notes within one octave on a keyboard.

Anacrusis. Note or notes preceding the first beat of a piece or phrase.

Antiphony. Performance by different singers/instrumentalists in alternation. Often – but not always – the different groups perform similar material.

Appoggiatura. An ornamental note that falls on the beat as a dissonance and then resolves by step onto the main note.

Articulation. The manner in which a series of notes are played with regards to their separation or connection – e.g. staccato (separated) or legato (connected).

Bebop. A style of jazz that developed in the 1940s from swing. More complex and less easy to dance to, it was characterised by improvisation, fast tempos, irregular phrase lengths and a greater emphasis on the rhythm section.

Cadence. A pair of chords signifying the end of a phrase in tonal music. *See also* **Imperfect cadence**, **Interrupted cadence** and **Perfect cadence**.

Cadenza. An unaccompanied showpiece for the soloist in a concerto.

Call and response. A pair of phrases, usually performed by different musicians, in which the second phrase is heard as a reply to the first phrase.

Chromatic. A chromatic note is one that does not belong to the scale of the key currently in use. E.g. in D major the notes F♮ and C♮ are chromatic.

Circle of 5ths. A harmonic progression in which the roots of the chords fall by intervals of a 5th (or rise by intervals of a 4th), e.g. D–G–C–F.

Comping. A term associated with jazz and popular music referring to the playing of a chordal accompaniment.

Concertino. The group of soloists in a Baroque **concerto grosso**.

Concerto. Most commonly a concerto is a work for one or more soloists (notably a pianist or violinist) with orchestra.

Concerto grosso. A type of music developed in the Baroque era using two distinct groups of instruments: a small group (the **concertino**) and a full orchestra (the **ripieno**).

Continuo. Short for 'basso continuo', the continuo instruments form the accompaniment in Baroque music. It may include instruments such as the harpsichord (capable of playing full harmony) and a cello or bassoon reinforcing the bass line.

Contrapuntal. Adjective to describe music that uses counterpoint. Counterpoint involves two or more melodic lines (usually rhythmically contrasted), each significant in itself, which are played or sung together at the same time.

Countermelody. An independent melody that complements a more prominent theme.

Counterpoint. *See* **Contrapuntal**.

Diatonic. A diatonic note is one that belongs to the scale of the key currently in use. E.g. in D major the notes D, E and F♯ are diatonic.

Diminished 7th. A four-note chord made up of superimposed minor 3rds.

Dissonance. Strictly speaking, any note not belonging to a triad in root position or first inversion. Some dissonances, particularly **suspensions** and **appoggiaturas**, add tension, which in early music had to be 'resolved'; others, notably **passing** and auxiliary notes, provide rhythmic and melodic decoration.

Dominant. The fifth note of a diatonic scale, e.g. C is the dominant of F.

Double stopping. The playing of two notes simultaneously on adjacent strings of a string instrument.

Exposition. The first section of a sonata-form movement, typically including the first subject in the tonic and the second subject in a related key.

Glissando. A slide from one pitch to another.

Harmonic rhythm. The rate at which harmony changes in a piece.

Homophonic. In a homophonic texture, one part has a melody and the other parts accompany, in contrast to contrapuntal writing, where each part has independent melodic and rhythmic interest.

Imitation. A contrapuntal device in which a distinct melodic idea in one part is immediately copied by another party, often at a different pitch, while the first part continues with other music.

Imperfect cadence. A cadence consisting of any chord usually I, ii or IV – followed by the dominant (V).

Interrupted cadence. A cadence most frequently consisting of chords V–VI, designed to defeat expectations by avoiding chord I.

Inversion (harmonic). When a chord has a note other than the root in the lowest part, it is an inversion. In a first-inversion chord the 3rd of the chord is in the lowest part, and in second-inversion chord the 5th. E.g. a triad of F major in first inversion is A–C–F, and in second inversion is C–F–A.

Inversion (melodic). When a melody line is heard upside down, e.g. pitches C–E–D are presented as C–A–B.

Leading note. The seventh note of a diatonic scale.

Lombardic rhythm. A reversed dotted rhythm with the shorter note first, e.g. semiquaver–dotted quaver.

Modulation. A change of key, or the process of changing key.

Mordent. A quickly played ornament which begins on the written note, moves up a step (upper mordent) or down a step (lower mordent) and then returns to the original note.

Motif. A short but distinctive musical idea that is developed in various ways in order to create a longer passage of music.

Ostinato. A repeating melodic, harmonic or rhythmic motif, heard continuously throughout part or the whole of a piece.

Passing note. A non-harmony note approached and quitted by step in the same direction, often filling in a melodic gap of a 3rd (e.g. A between G and B, where both G and B are harmony notes).

Pedal note. A sustained or repeated note, usually in a low register, over which changing harmonies occur.

Perfect cadence. A cadence consisting of the dominant chord (V or V^7) following by the tonic (I).

Pizzicato (pizz.). A direction to pluck (instead of bow) strings on a violin, viola, cello or double bass.

Polyphonic. This term has a similar meaning to **contrapuntal**, but tends to be used for vocal, not instrumental music.

Recapitulation. In sonata form, the section that follows the development. It is often closely based on the exposition, but normally both opens and closes in the tonic key.

Riff. A short, catchy melodic figure, repeated like an **ostinato** and commonly found in rock, pop and jazz.

Ritornello. In Baroque music, the repeated tutti section used as a refrain; most often in the first or last movement of a concerto, or in arias or choral works.

Rubato. The alteration of rhythm, particularly in a melodic line, by lengthening and shortening notes but keeping an overall consistent tempo.

Scat. In jazz, the singing of 'nonsense' sounds instead of words.

Sequence. Immediate repetition of a melodic or harmonic idea at a different pitch.

Sonata form. Typical first movement form of the Classical and Romantic periods. In three sections – exposition, development and recapitulation – often based on two groups of melodic material in two contrasting keys (first and second subject).

Sounding pitch. The pitch that sounds when a note is played by a transposing instrument. For example, when a B♭ clarinet plays a written C, the sounding pitch is a B♭.

Subdominant. The fourth note of a diatonic scale, e.g. F is the subdominant of C.

Suspension. A suspension occurs at a change of chord, where one part hangs on to (or repeats) a note from the old chord, creating a clash, after which the delayed part resolves by step (usually down) to a note of the new chord.

Swung rhythm. In jazz and other popular music, a certain freedom in performance whereby rhythms that might in other contexts be played 'straight' as equal notes are performed with the first of each pair longer than the second, often giving a kind of triplet effect.

Syncopation. Placing the accents in parts of the bar that are not normally emphasised, such as on weak beats or between beats, rather than in the expected place on strong beats.

Texture. The relationship between the various simultaneous lines in a passage of music, dependent on such features as the number and function of the parts and the spacing between them.

Tonality. The use of major and minor keys in music and the ways in which these keys are related.

Tonic. The first note of a diatonic scale, e.g. G is the tonic of G major.

Tremolo. A rapid and continuous repetition of a single note or two alternating notes.

Trill. An ornament consisting of a rapid oscillation between two adjacent pitches, usually for the duration of the ornamented note.

Triplet. A group of three equal notes played in the time normally taken by two notes of the same type.

Turn. A four-note ornament that 'turns' around the main note. It starts on the note above, drops to the main note, drops the note below and then returns to the main note.

Tutti. All instruments in an ensemble playing at the same time.

Unison. Simultaneous performance of the same note or melody by two or more players or singers.

Vibrato. A performing technique in which the pitch of a note wavers rapidly to give the sound greater vibrancy and resonance.

Walking bass. A bass line in which the notes are all on the beat, and move mainly by steps instead of leaps.